RCMP Training Academy
Regina, Saskatchewan Canada

TROOP 17

TROOP 17

The Making of Mounties

text by James McKenzie
photography by Lorne McClinton

Detselig Enterprises Ltd.

©1992 James McKenzie and Lorne McClinton

Canadian Cataloguing in Publication Data
McKenzie, James E.
    Troop 17

   ISBN 1-55059-039-1

    1. Royal Canadian Mounted Police. 2. Royal
Canadian Mounted Police—History. 3. Police training
—Saskatchewan—Regina. I. Title.
HV8157.M32 1992   354.710074   C92-091336-9

Detselig Enterprises Ltd. appreciates the financial assistance for its 1992 program from Alberta Foundation for the Arts and Canada Council.

All rights reserved. No part of this book may be reproduced in any form without permission in writing from the publisher.

Detselig Enterprises Ltd.
Suite 210, 1220 Kensington Rd. N.W.
Calgary, Alberta
T2N 3P5

Printed in Canada   SAN-115-0324   ISBN 1-55059-039-1

Acknowledgments

Dan Nugent and Bob Beaudoin worked closely with us all through this project, and we are especially grateful to them.

We also appreciate the assistance of Tony Antoniuk, Denis Arbez, Judy Best, Diane Brown, Dr. Orrison Burgess, Doug Casper, Francois Desfosses, Ernie Fast, Gary Faulconbridge, Ian Ferguson, Marilyn Frederiksen, Betty Glassman, Ruth Hoffart, Reg Jerrett, Maureen Jones, Pat Kamenka, John Keyuk, Henry Kinsella, Perry Kuzma, Bernie LaJoie, Marc Lavergne, Gilles Levesque, Mike Lynn, Bill MacRae, Sandy Mahon, Al Marshall, Terry Matatall, Yvon Mercier, Patricia Meyer, Glenn Miller, Gilles Moreau, Thelma Nugent, Gary Oberg, Dan Ouellette, Wayne Plimmer, Ed Plitz, Bob Ray, Wayne Ross, Dr. Bob Roy, Del Schumack, Barry Shannon, Bob Smart, Bill Spring, Jim Turner, Gill Vincent, Norm Wilson and Louis Wood.

We would also like to thank all the members of Troop 17. They are Dave Attew, John Babbitt, Keith Blake, John Christensen, Cathy Crow, Don Davidson, Mark Davidson, Brian Davison, Dave Dubnyk, Bob Fremlin, Kathy Furgason, Mark Gagnier, Wayne Gallant, Paul Gilligan, Garret Hoogestraat, Jason Kerr, Mel Klatt, Joe Kohut, Lorin Lopetinsky, Suzanne Lund, Trevor MacKay, Kerry Mah, Colette Perrier, Len Peters, Aaron Polk, Dave Rampersad, Ron Roberts, Marty Schneider, Mark Skotnicki, Dan Thorne, Dave Tyreman and Pat Zunti.

Although the Royal Canadian Mounted Police Training Academy has cooperated with the authors, the force does not necessarily agree with the contents.

Contents

Acknowledgments /5

Introduction /9

chapter one /15

chapter two /35

chapter three /57

chapter four /75

chapter five /93

chapter six /115

chapter seven /133

chapter eight /151

Introduction

Many men, and a growing number of women, aspire to become national icons. They apply to join the Royal Canadian Mounted Police. The RCMP has several thousand applications on file, with more pouring in every day, but most applicants don't make it because there are usually just a few hundred vacancies each year in the national police force. The RCMP has the luxury of picking the cream of the crop.

This is the story of thirty-two men and women who were among the chosen few. They had passed their written and physical examinations. Their reasons for wanting to join the force had been explored during probing interviews. Their pasts, right back to the time when they were in grade school, had been scrutinized. And finally, they had been sworn in as probationary constables.

The prize was within their grasp, but there was one more hurdle to overcome. They had to go through the RCMP Training Academy in Regina, Saskatchewan. Surviving the Academy is the price of admission to the RCMP. Mounties who had already done it told the newcomers that it was like six months in hell. The recruits quickly discovered that this was only a slight exaggeration.

Life at the Academy is rough. Recruits must work very hard to learn everything in a fairly short period of time; but that's not all. A lot more goes on than just basic police training. Passage through the Academy is also an initiation rite. Membership in the Royal Canadian Mounted Police is one of the closest things we have in this country to secular sainthood. Those who aspire to wear red serge must undergo a half-year of suffering and testing before they're elevated to the ranks of the elite force. They have to prove that they have the right stuff to be Mounties.

Sometimes the Academy is called the RCMP's boot camp. It has also been called the cradle of the force, because it's where "baby Mounties" are born, but more commonly it's referred to as Depot. The name dates back to the 1880s, when the North West Mounted Police, as they were then called, established an outpost and supply station along the banks of Wascana Creek. That depot soon became the frontier police force's headquarters. When the RCMP's administrative operations were transferred to Ottawa in 1920, Depot was retained as the national recruit training centre.

The Academy is the chief repository of the RCMP's heritage. The force's museum is on its grounds, and so is the monument honoring RCMP officers killed while on duty. The place has a definite military flavor. The flag is ceremoniously raised at the crack of dawn, and reveille sounds. Recruits sleep in barracks, thirty-two to a room, and they must double-time from class to class until they've earned their "marching orders."

In many ways, the place is a throwback to an era when the force had iron-fisted discipline. The RCMP kept a firm grip on the farm boys and adventurers who signed up for fifty cents a day. The force has become more liberal in its attitudes in recent years, but many of the old ways are preserved at the Academy. Modern recruits are older and more responsible than their predecessors, but they're still kept on a short leash, particularly at the start of training. Every aspect of their lives is tightly controlled, and they're expected to submit to authority without protest.

We met the thirty-two recruits featured in this book one Sunday evening in October 1990. It was the night before training began. They were a mixed lot. A few of them were the children of Mounties, following in their fathers' footsteps, but most were the first members of their families to have taken up police work. Some had dreamed of becoming Mounties since they were little kids, but many had tried other lines of work before deciding to give policing a whirl. Some had been accepted by the force soon after they applied because they belonged to "target groups" the RCMP wanted to attract. But many of them had waited six or eight years for vacancies to open up.

We followed this group, which was a typical cross-section of recruits entering the Academy in the early 1990s, through their six months of training. We monitored their progress through the long western Canadian winter to the following April, when, on a bright, warm Friday afternoon, they became the first troop to graduate in the Academy's 1991-92 fiscal year.

Making them into Mounties wasn't cheap. It cost the taxpayers about $1.3 million. That worked out to a little over $40,000 for each member of the troop, and covered everything from their salaries and those of their instructors to such things as uniforms, medical care and even the bullets they fired on the shooting range.

There were twenty-eight men and four women in the troop. They were from six provinces — British Columbia, Alberta, Saskatchewan, Manitoba, Ontario and Newfoundland. Some were from cities and towns, and others were country folks. Some were worldly, mature adults in their late twenties or early thirties, while others were kids of twenty-one or twenty-two. A few had served in the RCMP auxiliary or taken police-related courses at community colleges, but most had no previous experience with police work.

Some were tall, forceful men with moustaches; they looked like Mounties even before they put on their uniforms. Others were small and meek-looking; they didn't fit the stereotypical image of the burly police officer, and certainly didn't conform to the Hollywood version of the handsome, singing Mountie who "always gets his man."

A few recruits grew up with silver spoons in their mouths, but most were from working-class and middle-class homes. Many of them had been away from home for years, and so were used to running their own lives, but they adjusted with surprising speed to the strict discipline which the Academy imposed on them.

In fact, they showed a remarkable willingness to follow the rules and do whatever was demanded of them, no matter how pointless or stupid it seemed to be. When they were told they must spend hours each week shining their boots and ironing the bedsheets, they didn't question their superiors about the relevance of these activities to police work, they simply did them. When they were told they had to spend fifty hours learning foot drill, they accepted the explanation that it was good for them and would make them better Mounties.

After they had been at the Academy for a couple of months, they seemed to revert to the level of elementary school students. We wondered when they were going to put up their hands to ask if they could go to the bathroom. They seemed to be totally cowed by the corporals, writing down whatever they were told, accepting everything that was thrown at them without question or complaint.

We wondered if this highly respected, world-famous police training academy wasn't turning these fine young people into a bunch of robots. We feared that the Academy was churning out clone-like cops who blindly followed orders and had no personal sense of what is fair and reasonable, what is just, and what is right or wrong.

But after-hours discussions with many of the recruits revealed that their training was not brainwashing them. They were simply going along with the Academy's rules and regulations, and striving to meet its expectations because they realized they had no choice. It was apparent to them that they could not change the system, and there was no point in trying to buck it. They knew that boat-rockers would get the boot, and they didn't want that to happen.

The Academy's heavy schedule also played a large part in the recruits' behavior. They operated on automatic pilot. Weariness prevented them from giving much thought to anything other than what was required of them. It was like being on a treadmill that moved faster and faster. They had to run harder and harder, just to keep up, and didn't have time to think about anything else.

But underneath their tiredness and their apparent passivity and acceptance of the status quo, we were pleased to discover, their minds and their critical faculties were very much intact. When we sat down with the recruits privately, they told us what they really thought. They were well aware of the absurdity of some of the things they were subjected to, and quite conscious of the fact that they were playing a rather elaborate game. The RCMP was not turning them into automatons.

By talking to the instructors and administrators, we found that the Academy wasn't even trying to transform these bright, independent people into zombies, even if it gave them a temporary zombie-like existence for awhile. Rather, the idea was to impress upon them the need for discipline and teamwork, but ultimately to bring them to the point where they could take responsibility for themselves. The force hoped to mould them into the sort of Mounties who could go out on patrol alone, and conduct themselves competently and confidently through self-discipline, rather than through discipline imposed by others.

The Academy's strategy was to work them hard, to teach them the value of organization and time-management and to help them function at a high level of efficiency. The goal was to build them up physically and mentally, to give them a chance to discover what they could do, and to show them how much they could accomplish if they put their minds to it.

Most of the recruits came to understand that these were the Academy's goals, even if the methods used to achieve them were harsh and sometimes seemed hard to justify. But they also came to think of the Academy as an unreal place, a sort of a fantasyland, with its own strange rules and its own rigid logic. They saw the silliness of some of the rules, like the one forbidding them to wear blue jeans in their off hours, and they recognized the absurdity of punishments such as having to report to the guard room every hour, on the hour, for an entire weekend as punishment for some petty infraction.

They coped with the Academy's tough rules and strange ways by learning how to roll with the punches. They found that the best way to get along was to go along. They kept their mouths shut and did what they had to do, without worrying too much about whether it made sense. They argued that the RCMP had been training recruits this way for a lot of years, and the results were usually good. Who were they to tell the force how to do it? Who were they to say that the tried and true ways should be changed?

But that didn't mean they had to like it. They accepted it as a necessary and temporary evil, but most of them grew very tired of the Academy. As the end of training approached, they counted the days until they would escape the confines of boot camp and get out into the "real world" of police work when they were sent to their first postings in detachments across Canada.

chapter one

"This is not a university campus."

It's the night before their classes begin at the Royal Canadian Mounted Police Training Academy, and the recruits of Troop 17 don't look much like cops. Dressed in civilian clothes, they seem more like a bunch of university students, lounging around on a Sunday evening, killing time, swapping horror stories. Technically, they're already members of the force, and they hold the rank of constable. They've been sworn in and assigned their regimental numbers. They're even earning a pay cheque, but they have a long way to go before they earn the right to call themselves Mounties.

A lot of the chatter tonight centres around what's going to happen in their first drill class, scheduled for the following Thursday. Rumor has it that their drill instructor, a corporal named Ferguson, is a holy terror. He's said to be a tough bugger. He pounces on the slightest infraction of the rules, the tiniest imperfection in their dress or deportment. His first class will be a nightmare. He'll run them around the drill hall until their legs fall off. He'll make them do pushups until they can't lift their noses off the floor. He'll yell and swear and enjoy every minute of it.

Ferguson is reputed to be as unpredictable as an orangutan. One minute he's patiently explaining some point about drill, speaking in calm, reasonable tones, giving the impression that maybe he's not such a bad guy after all. And then, Wham! He turns mean. He centres out some poor recruit or punishes the entire troop. You never know where the guy is coming from.

But you can count on one thing. Ferguson's first drill class, scheduled for the last period on Thursday, will not end on time. When his allotted fifty minutes are up, this martinet will keep going. If his class runs into their supper hour, that's just too bad. He'll keep going until one of them passes out, or even better, until one of them throws up. If that unlucky person happens to be you, senior recruits have solemnly advised the newcomers, you should vomit into your hat. Ferguson will think that's admirable, and may take pity on you. If you're a total clod and puke on the floor, Ferguson will go nuts. He'll make you get down on your hands and knees and clean it up. And then, if he's really ticked off, he'll tell the other recruits to get the hell out of his sight, and he'll make you stay in the drill hall by yourself all night, polishing the huge wooden floor with a big tub of wax and a toothbrush.

Dave Rampersad laughs at that. He knows such stories are exaggerated. At least he hopes they are. He isn't sure, and that's part of the excitement as he and the thirty-one others in Troop 17 prepare to start their six months of training. Rampersad can't wait. "Ever since I applied to join the force," he says, "I don't think a day has gone by that I haven't thought about Regina, about how physically demanding and stern and strict it's going to be."

Rampersad is twenty-two. He was born in Trinidad, where his elementary school teachers practised the old British system of education. When students misbehaved or didn't have their homework done, the teacher whacked them with a cane. When Rampersad moved to Winnipeg as a teenager, he couldn't believe how lenient his Canadian teachers were. Despite the fact that he got used to the slack Canadian public and secondary school system, and then enjoyed even more liberalism when he went to university, Rampersad's mind nostalgically drifts back to the old days when he was a kid, and he knows that once again he will have to toe the line. He actually looks forward to it. "I enjoy discipline," he explains. He is especially eager to go to his first drill class with Corporal Ferguson, because that's where the discipline will be harshest. The tougher it is, Rampersad figures, the more he's going to get out of it. "All the talk doesn't scare me," he says with perhaps a bit too much bravado. "It just makes me want to get into it more . . . I want to break the ice and start doing it, even though I know it's going to be torture."

Corporal Ian Ferguson, Troop 17's drill instructor, is rumored to be a holy terror.

Rampersad doesn't know it yet, but he will soon get a belly full of discipline. What he endures at the RCMP Training Academy will make his days as a kid in Trinidad seem like a picnic. He will have such a hard time of it that he will telephone his mother and practically bawl his eyes out telling her that he doesn't think he can make it, and asking if she thinks maybe he shouldn't just come home and forget about becoming a Mountie. But that lies a few weeks ahead, and tonight Rampersad, like the others in Troop 17, is having a lot of fun talking about how tough it will be.

❖   ❖   ❖

When their training begins the following morning, Rampersad and the others feel a little let down. After all the hype, they discover that it isn't tough at all, at least not at the start. The formidable Ferguson's class isn't until Thursday, and before that happens, there's a nice, cushy orientation. Instead of being put through the mill, the recruits spend their time listening to the instructors talk about their subjects and explain what's coming in the months ahead.

Things began on a harsher note in the past when the Academy was more a school of hard knocks. There was no orientation in the 1950s and 1960s, before modern theories of education made their way into Depot. In the old days, you went to the pool on the first morning

The new recruits in Troop 17 in civilian clothes for their orientation.

and the instructor poked you with a bamboo stick and asked if you could swim. If you couldn't, he smiled sadistically and ordered you to jump into the deep end. After you had sputtered around for a minute or so, he sent somebody in to haul you out. That was how things were done through most of the Academy's history, which stretched back to 1882, when Canada's new national police force set up headquarters in Regina and started training recruits there.

But over the years, things had changed a lot, and orientation was one of the more recent innovations. Progressives said it was a change for the better, that it made sense to tell people what was expected of them, but traditionalists thought it was just one more way the Academy had gone soft. They liked the old ways which required recruits to either sink or swim.

It's Tuesday, day two of training. Orientation is nicely under way, and life is fairly casual. The recruits are in a classroom in B Block, one of the two dozen or so red-brick buildings that give the Academy the outward appearance of a university campus. The instructors who will be in charge of Troop 17's gym, swimming and self-defence class are talking to the recruits when Corporal Bernie LaJoie comes marching down the hall outside the classroom.

LaJoie is the division orderly, the "DO" for short. He's the Academy's roving butt-booter, the sergeant major's meany. LaJoie is the muscle when it comes to such things as how the recruits dress, how they behave and how they maintain their living quarters. LaJoie is a traditionalist. He doesn't like the way recruits are mollycoddled. He thinks respect is something that must be earned, not automatically accorded.

LaJoie floats like a bee, stinging recruits for the slightest offense. He knows all the rules, and he rejoices in his role as the enforcer. He sees himself as a key member of the school's training staff, but much to his displeasure, the higher-ups have decided otherwise. The Academy is down-playing discipline, and the DO's position is being cut. LaJoie is the last in a long line of corporals to hold the job. He's being transformed into a bureaucrat. His new title will be "support and administration NCO," and he will have to worry about mundane matters like base security and assigning beds. Soon there will be no more full-time ass-kicking for Bernie LaJoie.

His symbol of office, a leather pouch traditionally carried by the DO to hold a pencil and paper to record the names of misbehaving recruits, is being sent to the RCMP museum. LaJoie figures they might just as well ship him off to the museum too. He gripes that the elimination of the DO's post is just one more sign that the RCMP is going soft. "You can't order people around anymore," he complains. "It's the whole swing of the pendulum. Everything is human rights." The sergeant major, together with Ferguson and the other drill corporals, will still enforce the rules, he admits, but it won't be the same. They won't be able to devote their full time and attention to it. They won't play the role of roving nemesis, appearing from nowhere and arbitrarily doling out punishment. LaJoie thinks it's an important function, because it prepares the recruits for the uncertainty and unfairness they'll face as police officers.

"When I'm done with this job," he growls, "I want them to remember me as a dink, a real tough guy, but a person who was fair." In just a few weeks, his position will be officially abolished, but today he's still the DO, and for one of the last times, he's going to lay down the law to a new troop.

LaJoie waits impatiently outside the classroom while the physical education instructors complete their presentation. They have run overtime, but there's nothing LaJoie can do about it. He has a lot of power over the recruits, but he's only a corporal, the same rank as the other instructors. When they finally wind up their session, about ten minutes late, a couple of the recruits jump up and head for the classroom door, hoping to grab a soft drink or a smoke, but they don't get very far. "You're on my time now," LaJoie bellows as he strides into the room. The recruits meekly sit down as LaJoie carefully removes his cap, deliberately sets his swagger stick on the desk, and begins his lesson.

"This is not a university campus," he tells them, a look of disdain crossing his face, as if he has just smelled a foul odor. "There is no place here for free-thinking and individuality. You must dress as you are told and behave as you are told," he points out. He tells them they are now in a para-military organization and must accept a life of conformity and regimentation. The manuals are full of rules on how they must dress and behave, he says, but they must "give 110 percent." They must set an example when it comes to dress and deportment.

He says that nobody expects them to be perfect, but they must put forth "maximum effort and enthusiasm." The recruits sit silently, and respectfully take notes as he wades through the Academy's complex set of rules governing dress. It takes him about twenty minutes to cover them all.

Corporal Bernie Lajoie, division orderly. "This is not a university campus."

Then he explains the limits the Academy intends to impose on their freedom, not only while they are on the base, but also when they are off it. When they go shopping or drinking downtown, for instance, their civilian clothes must be neat and conservative. Jeans are forbidden. LaJoie says recruits are easy to spot on the street, not only because they're practically the only young people who aren't wearing jeans. "People will also recognize you easily by your haircut, the stunned look on your face, and the way you try to stay in step with your partner." He warns them that there are eyes everywhere. Any one of the Academy's 100 or so instructors might spot them committing an infraction. LaJoie reveals that he himself was recently at the West Edmonton Mall, hundreds of miles from Regina, and he saw some recruits who were not neatly dressed. They paid for this when they returned to the base. They were paraded before the sergeant major, who confined them to the base the following weekend.

LaJoie tells them that they must not only keep their hair short, but they must have it cut by the barbers at the Academy. A time will be designated for the troop to go to the barber shop, and they will report as ordered. "Sit in the chair, shut up, and let the barber cut your hair," he tells them, injecting a touch of humor into his voice and running his hand over his own balding pate. "I always ask for mine to be short on top," he jokes. He says the male recruits may grow a moustache, but it must be no more than one-eighth of an inch on either side of the mouth. He tells them that he has a "weed whacker" in his office for recruits with too much moustache, or with chest hair sticking out of the top of their shirts.

He tells them that if they break any of the rules, they may be "CBed" — confined to the base. That means not only losing their freedom to leave the Academy after classes and on weekends, but also having to dress in full uniform and report to the guard room every hour, on the hour. LaJoie says losing their freedom will be disappointing, but "training is to prepare you for disappointment. Sometimes it's 4:29 on a Friday and you're all set to get out of here, and then you get zapped, and you're CBed. If you can't live with that, maybe you shouldn't be a police officer."

He tells them they should avoid fights when they are off the base, even if punks try to provoke them and dare them to fight. "Why is my nose still straight after thirteen years of field work?" LaJoie asks. "Because I've got a good mouth, and I can talk my way out of fights." But he says the recruits are allowed to defend themselves if they have to — if, for example, they are jumped in a bar's washroom. He says that if they must fight, they should fight to win, but he recommends that they tell hostile people they've been in training for five months, "even if you've only been here for two weeks. They'll think you're trained in karate and all that other stuff, and they'll leave you alone."

LaJoie becomes philosophical. He says there are two types of people he can't stand — cheaters and liars. "When you make mistakes, own up to them," he advises the recruits. He tells them a story about a Mountie who had finished training and was serving in his first detachment, many years ago. This young hotshot roared out of the detachment parking lot one night in a police cruiser, screeching the tires because he thought it was fun. The next day, the sergeant in charge of the detachment asked the young Mountie about it.

"It would've been easy for this new member to lie and say that a car sped by, and he took off after it," LaJoie said. But the young Mountie told the truth, admitting that he had acted like a fool. "I know," said the sergeant, who unbeknownst to the young Mountie had seen the whole thing. "I saw what you did, Constable LaJoie." The recruits laugh when they realize the corporal has been talking about himself. He laughs along with them, and then brings home the point of the story. "Answer me honestly," he tells the new recruits. "Lie to me once and I'll have your ass on the parade square. If you make a mistake, admit your bloody mistake." He says that the Academy not only permits recruits to make mistakes, it expects recruits to make mistakes; but it also expects them to learn from those mistakes. "If you weren't going to make mistakes," he says reassuringly, "we'd just send you your uniform in the mail..."

It's 7:55 a.m. on Wednesday, the third day of training and the last day of orientation. The recruits are back in the same classroom, waiting for another instructor to arrive. They're still in civilian clothes, and despite what LaJoie has told them about the Academy not being a university campus, they still look like a bunch of college kids, and they're still gabbing away, just like they were on the first night. But the chatter ends abruptly when a trim, middle-aged man wearing a business suit walks into the room. One of the recruits yells "Troop!" and they all freeze.

Staff Sergeant Jim Turner, head of the Academy's standards section, acknowledges their gesture of respect with a nod, and he tells one of them to close the door. He says he has something to discuss with the troop, in private. He demands to know which one of them is Constable Polk. Aaron Polk, a meek-looking man, puts up his hand. Turner says it has come to his attention that Polk has recently been in "some kind of trouble" at the Original California Club. The OCC is a bar in downtown Regina that's popular with recruits. Polk was there one night and somehow got into a bit of a fight. The details aren't mentioned. Turner tells him he's lucky the incident happened before his training formally started, or he might have been kicked out of the Academy. Turner says he understands a second culprit was involved. Brian Davison immediately identifies himself. He looks even sorrier and mousier than Polk. Turner does not ask for their side of the story. He curtly orders them both to report to the guard room that night. "Next time anything like this happens," he warns them, "I can guarantee you won't stay in this troop."

Turner then begins his lesson. He tells the recruits that the force will treat them well if they stay out of trouble, but much more than that is expected of them. They must not just keep their noses clean. They must do their duty and show their loyalty to the RCMP. That's easy to say, he observes, but they might find it's not always so easy to do. For instance, they might have extra duties some weekend, and friends or relatives unexpectedly show up in Regina and want to visit. The recruit can ask to get out of his weekend duties, "but if you do, you'll reveal where your loyalties are," Turner says, suggesting that they're expected to put the RCMP ahead of personal convenience.

He assures them that they can all make it through training, but points out that it is not likely, and that a few may fall by the wayside. Only twice in the past two and a half years has every member of a troop of thirty-two gone all the way to the end, he notes. Usually one or two decide to quit. Either that, or they're backtrooped for such things as "poor attitude, poor performance or medical reasons." Backtrooping means being pulled out of your original class and placed in a troop at an earlier stage of training. In effect, it means repeating some of the course, and staying at the Academy for a few extra months.

Turner finishes by telling Troop 17 that the RCMP will get rid of them if they don't measure up, but they will be given the chance to leave "voluntarily." It will look better on their records than being dismissed. "We certainly don't want to ruin anybody for years to come," he says. But he also leaves them with a positive feeling. For all the talk about backtrooping and leaving the Academy, that's not the object of the exercise. The force has chosen them for training because they looked like good investments, and it wants them to make it all the way. "Our goal is to graduate you," Turner explains. "All you need is a certain attitude and application. We'll teach you everything you need to know to make it."

Corporals Del Schumack, Francois Desfosses and Bob Stewart (l-r) man the bridge. They watch for transgressions.

From the front, the drill hall looks like a barn, but twin turrets at the top of the old building give it a slightly castle-like appearance. Six Canadian flags flutter at the front entrance. When you walk through the door, you're a little surprised at what a big place it is — 80 feet wide and 200 feet long. The absence of pillars in the middle makes the floor space seem immense. There are wooden bleachers for spectators on either side of the entrance. Hanging from the ceiling are the flags of each of the ten Canadian provinces and two territories. Plaques bearing the provincial and territorial coats of arms adorn the walls. The hardwood floor is worn from the thousands of boots which have tramped over it each year.

Drill, both the kind done on horseback and the kind done on foot, goes back to the very beginning of the RCMP. The force was established in 1873 as a para-military outfit to bring law and order to the Canadian West. It started as a cavalry unit led by British-trained officers who were keen on spit and polish, discipline and a rigid chain of command. Over the years, the organization has evolved into a modern police force, but it has retained many of its military aspects. The very name of the subject taught in the drill hall, "dismounted calvary drill," is a reminder of the days when the mounted police rode horses, a practice which ended decades ago, except for ceremonial occasions and the RCMP Musical Ride. The Academy stopped giving recruits equitation training and sold off its horses in the mid-1960s.

Drill class roots go deep into the RCMP's cavalry past. Dismounted cavalry drill is its formal name. One object of the class is to get the members to move as a single unit.

A stuffed bison's head is mounted on one of the drill hall walls, and legends abound about what the old buffalo has seen over the years. There's one story about the recruit who fainted, got up and resumed marching, fainted again, got back up and marched some more, fainted again and so forth, six times in all. But by God, he finished the class, showing the kind of pluck that the RCMP likes to see in recruits. Then there was the recruit who was standing at attention during a drill class when a wasp landed on him. The recruit's natural instincts told him to brush the wasp away, but his drill training told him not to move because he was at attention. The recruit didn't flinch, and eventually the wasp flew away without stinging him. The recruit's drill instructor congratulated him for remaining still while he was at attention, and told him he would have received five days on guard duty if he had moved. Then the instructor put him on guard duty for ten days because the recruit was guilty of "stupidity." The instructor said that even though he was at attention, the recruit should have brushed the wasp away, "to avoid potential injury to government property."

But that, as they say, is history, and this Thursday afternoon the recruits of Troop 17 are standing in a more or less straight line in the middle of the massive drill hall. They're facing the bleachers and the front door. The appointed hour has arrived, and they silently wait for their encounter with the much-discussed Corporal Ferguson and the start of their first drill class.

Orientation is over. They're in uniform now, and bear some slight resemblance to Mounties, but their baggy brown pants mark them as rookies. They are also normally clad in unMountie-like running shoes, but they've taken them off and have put on the black boots that they're required to wear for drill class.

The troop leader, Pat Zunti, is on the far right of the line. He's called the "right marker," and despite his brown trousers, Zunti looks like a cop. He's six foot one, and weighs 210 pounds. He's also the oldest person in the troop. At thirty-three, it's unlikely that he could be mistaken for a college kid. Zunti is a muscular man and sports a big black moustache. He looks tough. His face seems to say, "I'll be nice if you're nice, but don't mess with me." Put a regulation RCMP uniform on him and a couple of stripes on his arm and Zunti could easily pass for a drill instructor himself, instead of a new recruit.

Next to Zunti is John Christensen, who also looks like a cop. Christensen is six foot five, weighs 235 pounds and is the biggest man in the troop. He also has a moustache, and knows more than most of his troopmates about the RCMP. His father is a retired superintendent, and his brother has been in the force for about ten years.

Standing third in line, next to Christensen, is Dave Dubnyk, a little shorter at six foot four, and slighter at 195. The next three men in the row are pretty well equal in height, all about six foot two, and so it goes, with the rest of the recruits stretched down the line, more or less in descending order of height, with quite a few of them topping six feet. Somewhere near the middle stands Jason Kerr. At twenty, Kerr is the baby of the troop. He hasn't attained the full girth of manhood, and weighs just 145 pounds. Kerr's slight build will soon win him the nickname of "Indian dog." He may be skinny, but he's worked on the oil rigs, and he's strong.

Ron Roberts, at an even six feet, is near the middle of the line. Roberts is twenty-eight, a Newfoundlander whose nickname is "Skipper." Roberts is balding and wears glasses. Put him in a business suit and you'd swear he was an accountant. Paul Gilligan is next. Gilligan in fact is an accountant. He thought he might like the profession, but after only a short time in the business, found he couldn't stand it and decided to become a Mountie. Len Peters is in there, too. He used to be a prison guard, but got tired of the job and decided to join the RCMP.

A bit further down is Suzanne Lund, the first of the four women in the line. She's blonde, tall and slim, with an excellent figure which even her baggy brown pants and loose-fitting uniform shirt don't hide. Next to Lund is Dave Rampersad. Rampersad's black skin and his pot belly make him stand out from the crowd. Next to Rampersad is Kerry Mah, another recruit whose appearance catches the eye. In his case, it's because he's oriental. Mah and Rampersad have already started to make jokes in their off-duty hours about being the only "visible minorities" in the troop.

A little further down the line is the troop's second female member, Cathy Crow. Crow has short brown hair and a cheerful look, almost as if she is expecting to enjoy herself in drill class. She is five foot seven and weighs a hefty 170 pounds. Crow knows she is not as physically fit as she might be, but she used to be the director of a high school marching band, and she thinks this will help in drill class.

Brian Davison, one of the scoundrels involved in the infamous incident at the Original California Club, stands next in line. At five foot six, he's the shortest male in the troop, but Davison is a wiry 155 pounds. Years of athletics, especially skiing, have made him a very fit young man, and despite his diminutive stature, he doesn't look like a person you would want to tangle with.

Finally, there are the last two members of the troop. Both are much smaller than the rest, and both are female. Kathy Furgason is five foot three and although she weighs 135 pounds, she looks lighter. Her short hair and pert features give her somewhat of a tomboy look, and the uniform does nothing to increase her femininity. At the end of the line is Colette Perrier, who is just five foot two and weighs only 120 pounds. Perrier's face has an alert, vivacious quality, seeming to say that she may be little, but she can hold her own in this or any other crowd. But in the company of so many taller and heavier companions, she looks particularly small and vulnerable. It's hard to imagine Perrier getting the better of anybody in a bar fight.

A warm prairie wind drifts through the front doors of the big building, providing the nervous recruits with a welcome breeze. Five minutes crawl by as they stand in their long single row and wait. A dozen or so spectators have gathered to watch, and they're sitting in the bleachers, also eyeing the clock.

The sound of his heavy boots slamming rhythmically down on the shiny wooden floor heralds the arrival of the man who, more than any of their other instructors, will influence Troop 17. A troop's drill instructor does a lot more than teach them drill and give them a hard time in class. He decides when they can get rid of the baggy brown pants and the running shoes and start dressing like real Mounties. He says when they can march around the base instead of jog. He decides who their right marker will be. He inspects their barracks. He nails them when they have anything wrong with their uniform, or when they step out of line in any one of a countless number of ways.

Corporal Ian Ferguson does not simply march into the drill hall. He makes an entrance from behind the bleachers. His hat is perfectly positioned, exactly two fingers above his nose. He stands six foot one, but his boots make him a couple of inches taller. His creaseless brown tunic covers his fit, muscular frame. Three stars on his sleeve show he has fifteen years of service with the force. His sleeve also bears crossed rifle and pistol badges, with a crown above, showing that he is an expert shot. His blue trousers with the distinctive RCMP yellow stripe billow out of the top of his high brown boots at a rakish angle. His boots, set off by gleaming silver spurs, glisten with a rich, warm shine. Ferguson wears brown gloves and carries a three-foot swagger stick, which he snaps from his right hand to under his left arm as he halts in front of Pat Zunti, the right marker.

Corporal Ian Ferguson doesn't march into drill hall. He makes an entrance.

Zunti holds out the clipboard. Ferguson grabs it. The board lists the names of the members of the troop, but Ferguson seems to have no time for such trivial matters. He hurls the metal clipboard contemptuously across the floor, sending it skittering to the edge of the bleachers with a loud clatter. The corporal obviously has a wicked temper, which can apparently be triggered by absolutely nothing. Maybe all those tall tales about this guy are true after all.

Ferguson reveals what is bothering him. He points out sarcastically that the troop is supposed to be standing in order of descending height, but some people are out of place. Ferguson shakes his head in disgust. He wonders out loud whether Zunti is very bright, if he cannot do something as simple as line up his troop properly. "Are you drunk today, Zunti?" he asks. Zunti says he is not. Ferguson goes down the line, moving various members of the troop from place to place, until he is satisfied that they are perfectly arranged, according to height. Then he orders them to "number off from the left," and he stands glaring at them as they count off, until they reach Colette Perrier, who shouts "Thirty-two!" Somehow they have managed to get that right, but the instructor gives them no credit for it.

Crossed rifles and pistol badges with a crown on top indicate Ferguson is a crack shot. His swagger stick or drill cane is his badge of office.

"Are you drunk today, Zunti?" Corporal Ferguson adjusts the line of recruits.

Ferguson says he wants those with odd numbers to step one pace forward, and those with even numbers to step one pace back. He explains that this will put them in what is known as "troop formation." He gives them the command, but when they move to their new places there's a slight mix-up. Two of the taller men have somehow ended up standing next to each other in the back row. Ferguson demands to know how this could have happened. He determines that somehow, both of the men in the back row think they are number eight. Ferguson ridicules them for being so stupid. He discovers which one has made the mistake, and tells the culprit he must pay for his mistake by doing ten pushups. When the recruit hesitates a second, Ferguson bellows at him, "Why isn't your ass out here?" The recruit skitters into a prone position in front of troopmates, but he doesn't move quickly enough to suit the demanding corporal.

"I want you people to follow instructions at all costs," Ferguson shouts. He orders them all to do ten pushups. Then he tells them to "touch all four walls" of the drill hall. If they had been thinking clearly, they might simply have run across the floor on a diagonal, going to one corner and simultaneously touching both the north and west walls of the big hall, then crossing the floor kitty-corner to touch both south and east walls in the other corner. But the recruits are not thinking that fast. There's a mad dash, and the recruits are running in all directions at once, like a pack of terrified dogs scattering when their master opens the kennel gate. Some run to the west wall, others to the east, and in no time there are recruits going every which way. When they've all touched each of the four walls and returned to their places in troop formation, Ferguson demands ten more pushups. When some of them are slow in finishing that exercise, he complains that time is being wasted. Trevor MacKay, one of the younger recruits, smiles. Ferguson pounces on him. "Wipe that stupid grin off your face," he says, ordering MacKay to do an extra ten pushups.

Since their hats were not properly positioned, Mel Klatt lost his hat and Brian Davison had to wear his backwards for the remainder of drill class.

"Monkey see, monkey do; drill is a conditioning process." — Ferguson.

Then Ferguson goes back to his lesson. Once again, he tries to get them to move from a single line into the two-tiered troop formation. Once again he has them array themselves according to height and count off by numbers. When Ferguson gives the command, the odd-numbers move one step forward and the even numbers move one step back. They screw it up again. This time there are two number twenty-eights. Ferguson is really steamed. He demands ten more pushups from everyone, and then orders them to perform a new physical exercise. This one is called "five-to-ones." They must run to the far end of the drill hall, do five pushups, run to the other end of the hall and do four pushups, and keep running back and forth until they've worked their way down to one pushup.

And so it goes. Ferguson tries to teach them some of the basics. He alternates between giving them instruction and making them do physical exercises. They soon discover that it doesn't matter who slips up. They must all pay for the mistake. Ferguson's tone of voice shifts from firm, when he is trying to teach them something about drill, to harsh, when he chews them out for screwing up. Sometimes he deals with them as a group, and sometimes he picks on individuals. The weak ones draw his attention, and he is particularly tough on those who are getting tired, or are not well coordinated when they march. He hops on Ron Roberts, for instance, because he has trouble staying in step. But the one he really goes after is Cathy Crow. He orders her to stand in the rear rank "because you're too fat to be in the front rank." He calls her "butterball" and tells her to eat less and exercise more, and says that if she does that, "you'll find there's a healthy, skinny person in there that wants to get out."

Cathy Crow, red-faced with exertion, bears the brunt of Ferguson's displeasure.

Sweat is soon showing through many of the recruits' shirts, but Crow is the worst. She is perspiring so much it looks like she has been standing in the shower. The strong recruits are able to keep up with the punishing pace, and some seem to be thriving on it, but the weaker ones can't keep up, and poor Cathy Crow suffers the most. Her excess weight and general lack of physical fitness cause her to fall further and further behind the rest of the troop. She is the weakest physical link in the troop, a fact that becomes more and more apparent as the class continues.

Ferguson really digs into her. He demands to know how she got into the RCMP, and he complains about the selection system which permits a person in such poor condition to be admitted to the Academy. The teaching and the exercises continue, but finally there comes a point where Crow is unable to do another pushup. When Ferguson yet again orders them all to "get down and give me ten," Crow collapses onto her stomach. She makes a valiant but futile effort to push herself up on her arms. She drags herself to her feet when the others have done their pushups.

The class is scheduled to end at 4:30, but when that time comes, Ferguson ignores the clock. He keeps them marching, and then he makes them run and do more pushups. It goes on until several of them, like Crow, do not seem to be able continue. They look like they're ready to drop, and even the strongest no longer seem to be having fun. It is at this point, when the clock almost reaches five, that it finally, mercifully ends. Ferguson dismisses them contemptuously. "Get out of here," he shouts, and tired as they are, they obey with vigor. They run off the drill floor, take off their boots, put on their running shoes, and get out of that drill hall and out of Corporal Ferguson's sight as quickly as possible. Even Crow manages to find the strength to flee quickly.

After they are gone, Ferguson talks about what has just gone on with Troop 17. He feels he has made a good beginning with this new group of recruits. "I'm not here to make anybody cry or throw up under stress or out of anxiety, although certainly that happens from time to time," he says. "You want to be aggressive, but not excessively harsh. You want to gain their respect." He sees drill as a conditioning process. He shows the recruits what to do, and then he makes them practise until it's almost automatic. Ferguson calls it "monkey see, monkey do." He has a goal. By the end of their training, he hopes they will be able to execute a fifteen- or twenty-minute drill routine which includes all the basic marching movements. He hopes they will be able to do it in front of their instructors and the Academy's top brass, and in front of their friends and relatives. He hopes they will make a good show at graduation.

But that's six months down the line, and between now and then, a lot more than marching will be going on in the drill hall. Ferguson says part of his job is to be a role model. He sets an example of how a Mountie should dress, how he should march, and how he should conduct himself generally as a police officer. Ferguson wants his firm, self-confident manner to rub off on the recruits. "You can't appear to be afraid of any given situation. You've got to take command. When you approach a loud house party, you can't walk up quietly and gently tap on the door. The neighbors want the police officer to do something, so you've got to show some aggressiveness, some authority. People come in here very timid to start with, and gradually they gain a measure of confidence."

Ferguson says another part of his job as the troop's drill instructor is to help the recruits learn self-control. In a way, he's a stand-in for the punk who tries to aggravate the police officer. Mounties have to learn to keep their cool, to remain firm and calm when they are provoked. Ferguson provides them with plenty of provocation, and if they can handle what he dishes out, they should be able to handle what the public throws at them.

He says there are lines he doesn't cross. For instance, he doesn't strike the recruits with his swagger stick, and in fact he doesn't touch them at all, unless it's with a gentle hand to draw attention to an undone button, or to show them where he wants them to stand. But he moves in on them in an intimidating manner, shoving his face to within a couple of inches of theirs, invading their body space and rattling them without actually assaulting them.

"I'm not here to make anyone cry." — Ferguson.

He swears occasionally, but keeps it to a minimum. Ferguson says the Academy's policies have changed since he was a nineteen-year-old recruit in 1971. Drill instructors then used a good deal of profanity, justifying it on the grounds that it would prepare recruits for what they were going to hear on the streets. But Ferguson doesn't swear much. He says a lot of cursing by the instructor "creates an unprofessional impression," and he has found that the same results can be achieved by using other words. "It's the format in which you are addressed. There's a difference in the inflection and the delivery, and that's more important than the actual words which are spoken."

Ferguson says drill has another purpose. It helps the recruits learn to work together. Drill forms the basis of training for "tactical units," commonly know as riot squads, where teamwork is essential. "You don't just run into a mob with the truncheons flying," Ferguson points out. "You have to have a lot of discipline. It's a controlled show of force. If you march up in a disciplined show of strength, nine times out of ten the rioters will disperse."

After supper that night, some of the recruits are discussing their session with Ferguson. Mark Gagnier, who is in good physical condition, has already bounced back from the strenuous workout. "Everything I heard is true," says Gagnier, who is twenty-eight years old and worked on an automobile assembly line in Windsor for several years before joining the force. He sees drill as part of the Mountie-building process, and accepts it without question. "It's tough, really tough," Gagnier says, "but you're here to learn to be a cop. That's the career you chose, and you've got to put up with what goes on around here."

Lorin Lopetinsky is just twenty-one, and admits to being a little afraid during the drill class. He says he was intimidated not so much by the yelling or by the physical punishment, but because his success as a recruit rests in the hands of a man like Ferguson. "A man who walks out in an impeccable uniform with a stick in his hand, a tall man with boots that go 'click click click' on the floor. You're standing there in brown pants, and you know nothing. This man comes out and starts barking orders at you, screaming at you, throwing the clipboard. Fear just sets in, like, O my God, look at this man. He's insane. It's a fear that you don't want to screw up in front of a whole bunch of people. You don't want to have to get down and do a whole bunch of pushups. It's embarrassment and fear. It's like you're back in high school, and you're in front of the principal again."

Trevor MacKay is also just twenty-one, but he doesn't take things as seriously as Lopetinsky does. MacKay bubbles with excitement and says he had a lot of fun during the class. He knows he was supposed to be intimidated, but he found the whole thing kind of funny. He expresses mock fear about the forty-nine drill classes still to come. "I don't know whether I'm supposed to laugh or not," he says, "and I don't want to get into trouble for laughing all the time in drill class."

chapter two

"I'm not running away with my tail between my legs."

Eight days after Troop 17's first drill class, Cathy Crow sat in an east Regina coffee shop, smoked a few cigarettes, and relaxed. It was Friday night. She had signed out on a weekend pass and rented a motel room so she could snooze, watch TV, and enjoy the luxury of showering in private. She and the other recruits had completed their second week of training, and so far Crow had found it pretty tough. She hoped that getting away from the Academy for a couple of days would make her feel better.

Because of her poor physical condition, Crow was having a hard time in her "physical classes." Four subjects — gym, self-defence, swimming and drill — made up about thirty-five percent of the training program. The rest was academic and practical work. Recruits called their grueling physical classes "the big four," and when all four were on the schedule, even the fittest members of the troop were worn out at the end of the day.

Crow said she was tired, but she felt the Academy was right to put her through the tough physical program. She knew that police work required a lot of stamina, and that six months of intense exercise would build her up. She also thought it was better to discover her physical limitations while she was still in the safe environment of the Academy, rather than later, when she was out in a detachment and was called upon to break up a bar fight or get into some other physical confrontation.

"At least I'll know what to do in certain situations," she said. "Whether I'm capable of doing it or not is another question, but at least I'll know what to do." She was determined to become physically fit, and believed the Academy's compulsory training program would provide the incentive she needed to get in shape. Some people are naturally inclined toward vigorous exercise, she observed, but unfortunately, she wasn't one of them. "I need a push," she said.

Although she had already lost five pounds, she was still flabby. Crow felt she was about as fit as "the average person on the street," but this wasn't nearly good enough to make it through training, and she knew she had a long way to go. Corporal Ferguson had asked her how someone as unfit as she had managed to get into the Academy. The answer was that while the RCMP had a long and thorough selection process, its physical standards were low, especially for women. Crow was able to get into the force by performing a few undemanding exercises, and even then she just made it past the minimum.

"I know I didn't score high on the fitness test to get in here," the twenty-seven-year-old Crow admitted. "My cardiovascular system was pretty good because I was doing a lot on the exercise bike, but it wasn't fantastic. I had to do some pushups. I know I'm not a superstar. Their acceptance formula is based on a point system, which takes into account a lot of factors besides physical condition. There are other things they want from me. They knew I wasn't in good shape when they hired me."

Crow had never been athletic, but she was used to hard work. She grew up on a farm near North Pelham in Ontario's Niagara Peninsula. While studying sociology and psychology at Brock University in St. Catharines, she held down two jobs. She was director of the marching band at her old high school, and she also worked as a probation officer. She married while still in university, and planned to be a "happy housewife," but after a couple of years, the marriage went sour. When she saw that a divorce was inevitable, Crow started working in a detention home for young offenders, and set about finding herself a career.

She applied to both the Ontario Provincial Police and the RCMP. In many respects, Crow was a good candidate. She was intelligent, well educated and had related experience. She was also female — an advantage since both police forces were trying to attract more women. She preferred the RCMP because she thought the training was better. Ironically, it was the extra emphasis the Mounties put on physical conditioning that was most attractive to her. Corporal Ferguson had been right when he told Crow that inside her unfit, over-weight body there was a healthy, thin person struggling to come out. She wanted to be fit, and she thought the Academy was the place to get fit. She hadn't realized how demanding it was going to be, and how much easier it would have been if she had got in shape before beginning her training.

After she was accepted by the RCMP and sworn into the force, Crow was sent to Montreal for eight months to study French. The RCMP values bilingualism, and Crow did well at it. She achieved three "B" levels, meaning she was bilingual in reading, writing and speaking. It was a good start to her career. The federal police force, like other arms of the national government, prefers its members to speak both of Canada's official languages.

Crow was encouraged to get into better physical shape in Montreal, but found that she was so busy learning French, she had little time for physical activity. A twice-weekly fitness program in Montreal was compulsory, but she didn't benefit much from it. By the time she arrived in Regina, she was carrying 170 pounds on her five-foot-seven frame.

She continued to have trouble in drill. Thanks to her experience with the marching band, she didn't have a problem performing drill movements, but when Corporal Ferguson made the troop run and do pushups, Crow was the last one to finish, and she was usually sweating heavily by the end of the class. In the pool, she had no trouble with the swimming, but she ran into problems when she had to physically exert herself. In one of the classes, the instructor ordered the recruits to do a vigorous exercise known as "ins and outs." They had to jump into the water, grab the side of the pool and hoist themselves out, plunge back in, lift themselves back out, and so on, twenty-five times in all.

"Crow was stuck and she was just hanging there," recalled Joe Kohut, one of her troopmates. "Once we hit twenty-five, we all stopped. The instructor asked who didn't do twenty-five, and Crow screamed that she couldn't get out of the pool. The corporal said until she gets out of the pool, everybody back in. I think that's the day we did something like sixty-five 'ins and outs.' I don't know if she was hurt or simply tired. She was just hanging on the side of the pool."

Crow recalled the agony she went through, both physically and mentally. "I had zero strength left. The last one was so hard. Afterwards, I felt so bad because they all had to work so much harder because of me." Requiring the others to do extra exercises was known as "making the troop pay" for a weak member. It was a strategy employed by instructors to bring peer pressure to bear on weaker individuals. The idea was that the troop was only as strong as its weakest link. The person at the bottom would work especially hard to shape up, so that the rest of the troop wouldn't have to keep "paying" for his or her inadequacies.

The strategy had worked well over the years when all the recruits were male, but it had limited effectiveness in Crow's case since she lived in a different building than her male troopmates. She was in a dorm with the other three women from Troop 17 plus women from several other troops. Crow rarely saw the men in her troop outside of classes, so the effect of peer pressure was minimal.

But there were times when it did play a significant part, and seemed to help Crow. One day in self-defence class the recruits had to crawl the length of the gym floor on their bellies, using only their elbows to propel them. Everyone else finished, but Crow still had more than halfway to go. The troop started shouting and clapping, urging her on. Then Pat Zunti, the right marker, ran back and joined Crow on the floor. Another recruit ran back, and another, until they were all down on their bellies crawling with her until she made it to the end.

Crow's instructors often gave her "mandatories," which were additional exercises after classes, but usually she didn't do them. Her physical education instructor, for instance, put her on "mandatory pushups," which meant she was supposed to do an extra 500 pushups over the course of the following week. But Crow couldn't do them because she had pulled a groin muscle when she slipped on the ice while marching to class.

And so it went. She stayed at the bottom of the class in the physical courses, and continually had mandatories, but she also had physical and medical problems which prevented her from doing the exercises. She suffered from pulled muscles, strains and a variety of other ailments which incapacitated her. Most of the recruits had troubles like this from time to time, but Crow almost never seemed to be free of them. She often went to the Academy's medical treatment centre, and the doctor would put her on "Mod B," which meant she was excused from the most rigorous aspects of training. While the others in the troop ran, did pushups or ins and outs, Crow often sat on the bench. While they wrestled in self-defence class, Crow stood at the side, watching.

Once she was off Mod B, she would try to exercise, and again would hurt herself or some other physical problem would crop up. As the weeks rolled by, she fell further and further behind. The others in the troop grew stronger and took on increasingly greater physical challenges, but Crow virtually stood still. She wasn't happy about this, but she wasn't worried about being removed from training or kicked out of the Academy because of her poor physical performance.

She said she had heard a lot of talk about that sort of thing among the other women in the dorm, but "ninety percent of them are empty threats. The only time they will actually throw you out is if you don't try. This is terrible to say, but they've invested a lot of money in me, and I don't think they're going to get rid of me that easily."

Crow's assessment turned out to be accurate for quite awhile. For almost three months, she continued to have trouble with the physical side of training, but she kept up with her academic classes, and she remained in Troop 17. But gradually, as she fell further and further behind in the physical classes, she began to lose the sympathy and respect of most of the other members of the troop. Many of the people who had supported Crow at the beginning, and who had crawled along beside her and urged her on during the first weeks of training, eventually began to question whether she was trying hard enough. They wondered whether she was trying to coast through training, and they began to make snide remarks about her lack of fitness, seeing her as an outsider rather than as one of them.

They spoke about "losing respect" for her, and not wanting to have her as a police partner after graduation — the ultimate insult. Winning the respect of fellow-recruits and instructors was of prime importance at the Academy. Although you might not be as strong or as fast as others in the troop, as long as you tried your best and strived to reach your full potential, you were respected.

Crow lost the respect of her troopmates. They questioned whether she belonged at the Academy, and several of them questioned the system that let her in, and let her remain in the troop. They wondered why the people in charge were letting Crow "get away with it." They were expected to meet high standards. Why wasn't Crow expected to meet them too?

Cathy Crow struggles with situps. "I know I'm not a superstar . . . There are other things they want from me. They knew I wasn't in good shape when they hired me."

They wondered whether standards were so low that she might graduate from the program without having to suffer the discomfort they were suffering. They wondered, in short, whether Crow was going to "slip through the cracks."

Publicly, they didn't let on that it was bothering them, preferring to preserve the appearance of group unity, especially in front of their instructors. They made a great show of togetherness. One of them would call out, "Who's the best troop?" and they would all respond with a vigorous, "Troop 17!" They knew that their instructors liked such demonstrations of unity and spirit. They had also been told repeatedly that it was the troop's collective duty to help its weakest members, but after awhile, nobody seemed willing to help Crow.

She had few friends in the troop, and while many of the others were pairing up and getting in extra practice in the pool and the gym, Crow stayed pretty much to herself.

Some people in the troop began to feel bitter about always having to "pay" for Crow, and imagined that she actually enjoyed seeing them do extra exercises because of her. The other women in the troop became especially critical. "In PT when she fell off the bar she was laughing because we had to do twenty double jack-knifes and twenty double-squats," complained Kathy Furgason, who was in good shape and had few problems with physical training. "We were all trying to cheer her on," said Colette Perrier, who was also in good condition, "but I've never seen her cheer anybody else or try to help anyone else. You ask her to do you a favor or something, and she's always too busy. She's totally separated herself from the rest of the troop."

It wasn't pleasant for Crow. She had little sympathy from her troopmates and she was falling further and further behind, and eventually, the Academy's quality-control system caught up with her, too. As the troop's training progressed, each recruit was required to meet specific performance objectives. For example, they had to run the 1.5-mile "Cooper's Test" in a certain amount of time, depending on their age and sex. Such targets were known as "benchmarks." If a recruit failed to make a benchmark, the standards office was informed. Crow missed several benchmarks, and consequently her instructors wrote up reports pointing this out and detailing her lack of progress. Crow was called into the standards office and given formal notice that she was not meeting the requirements.

Her troopmates wondered whether she would return to the Academy after the ten-day Christmas break, and for awhile, Crow considered not returning. When she was at home for the holiday, she suffered a lot of pain in her ribs. Sometimes it was so bad that she had trouble sleeping.

But Crow was determined to succeed if she could, and hard as it was for her to do, she came back to Regina after Christmas. But things just didn't get any better. A couple of weeks later, as Troop 17 reached the halfway point in its training, Crow was again called into the standards office, and this time she was told that she had fallen too far behind the rest.

She was taken out of Troop 17. She was moved out of the women's dorm and was given private accommodation in C Block. She was put on a special weight-loss diet and was no longer required to go to class, but each morning and afternoon she went to the gym and did exercises under the supervision of a corporal. When she wasn't in the gym, she performed routine duties such as issuing uniforms to new recruits. She remained on this special program for about two months, and then she was put into another troop and given a second chance to make it through training. But her difficulties continued, and eventually she left her new troop, too, and left the Academy and the RCMP without graduating.

The RCMP didn't give up easily on Cathy Crow. The force's efforts to keep her in the training program as long as possible and to help her get into good physical shape were a far cry from the way things used to be done at the Academy. Previously, people who couldn't keep up with the demands of training were given a curt ultimatum: shape up or pack your bags and go home. In most cases, they were pressured to resign. Their instructors would give them such a hard time that they had little choice but to quit.

One former self-defence instructor, Staff Sergeant John Keyuk, recalled that he had a method of dealing with "a little rolly-polly who would drag the whole troop down. I would initiate a negative motivator that would make them very, very tired. Pushups, runs, sprints, more pushups. The reason behind it would be brought to their attention." This would lead to intense peer pressure, and sometimes ostracism. Occasionally some troopmates would pack a recruit's bags and set them out in the middle of the parade square. It was a broad hint that the troop had decided it was time for him to go.

Such treatment contrasted sharply with the new approach that saw the Academy helping people like Crow, rather than simply punishing them or getting rid of them. Traditionalists and hard-liners said this new, more compassionate way of dealing with recruits was a waste of time and money, but others felt it was about time the Mounties started helping recruits who were having difficulties instead of wasting their potential. The new procedure in such cases was to systematically document the recruit's inadequacies, and take steps to help them succeed, if at all possible. Only after that had been done would dismissal be considered. The force bent over backwards to try to save Crow's career. Interestingly, few of her former troopmates were willing to go that far. By the time she left Troop 17, most of her colleagues were glad to see her go.

"She got what she deserved," said Kathy Furgason. "She didn't try in anything." Colette Perrier was even more blunt. "Everybody else here has been working their asses off and working with injuries and just pushing it and pushing it," she said. "Crow hasn't done anything. There's no way she should get through this place unless she changes her attitude."

Suzanne Lund was also unsympathetic. "I wasn't heartbroken about it," said Lund. "She wasn't ready for this, and I wouldn't trust her as a partner." Lund said she had nothing against Crow personally, "but you have to look at people here as potential partners, and if I can't trust someone to be my partner or someone else's partner, I wouldn't want them in here. Your life could depend on it someday, and this goes beyond friendship. It sounds cruel, but it's a fact of life."

Lund also came under a lot of pressure during her training, but unlike Crow, she was able to overcome her difficulties, or at least survive them. Lund's troubles were not physical. She was younger, taller, slimmer and stronger than Crow, and she had no trouble keeping up with the Academy's physical demands. Lund's problems centred around matters of a more intellectual and emotional nature — having to take responsibility, and having to cope with male chauvinism.

At the end of the troop's third week of training, Lund was fitting into the training program nicely. But then she was suddenly thrust into a leadership position. She became Troop 17's "right marker," taking the place of Pat Zunti, the oldest man in the troop, a popular guy who had been chosen by his troopmates at the start of training as the right marker and troop leader. It happened suddenly and unexpectedly. The troop was in drill class and, as often happened, something was wrong with the way they performed a drill movement. As usual, Corporal Ferguson unleashed a blast of criticism, but this time he announced that Zunti was too muscle-bound and uncoordinated to be the right marker, so he was going to replace him. Ferguson turned around and, seemingly out of the blue, picked Lund.

"I came to drill a bit late," Lund recalled. "I had been at the physiotherapist's office, and I was standing by the bleachers waiting for Corporal Ferguson to halt the troop and turn around and yell at me. He told Zunti to get out and me to get in there." Lund sprinted to Zunti's place in the front rank on the far right, the right-marker's spot. It was the key position for coordinating the troop's drill movements. Lund, who was tall (five-foot-ten), slim (130 pounds) and well coordinated, was a good marcher, and she did a good job in the right marker's spot for the rest of the class.

"I thought I was just being used as a demonstration or something," she recalled later. "But when the class finished, Pat came up and handed me the clipboard. Pat said to me, 'You're it,' and I said, 'I don't want to be it.' He said, 'Neither did I, but now it's you.' At first we all kind of laughed about it. We heard Ferguson was teaching Pat a lesson, and that Ferguson has never had a female right marker, and I wouldn't last very long. Pat would be back, or some other guy would be in. And so for the first while I had the job, it was almost a little bit of a joke. Nobody took it seriously, including myself."

That turned out to be a mistake, as Lund eventually learned. Ferguson's apparently casual action in replacing Zunti with Lund had major implications for the troop. If the right marker's post had only involved guiding the troop through its movements in the drill hall, Lund wouldn't have had anything to worry about. She was good at that. But the job entailed a lot more. It was also an organizational and leadership position.

The right marker was in charge of the troop and was responsible for such things as making sure the recruits got to class on time and troop discipline. It was up to the marker to keep the troop in line when the corporals weren't around, and as Lund found out, that wasn't always easy, especially when she was female and most of the troop was male. The right marker also made decisions about such things as which items of clothing the recruits would wear on certain occasions. On semi-warm days, for instance, would jackets be worn or not? Such decisions were important, because the recruits had to be uniformly dressed, or they would all get into trouble with the corporals. In addition, the marker was supposed to call meetings, organize drill practices and speak for the troop when it had dealings with superiors.

It was a key job, requiring a firm hand and good management skills. Having all that responsibility dropped on her put Lund in a difficult position. Her failure to take a firm hold of the job soon caused her and the other recruits a lot of problems.

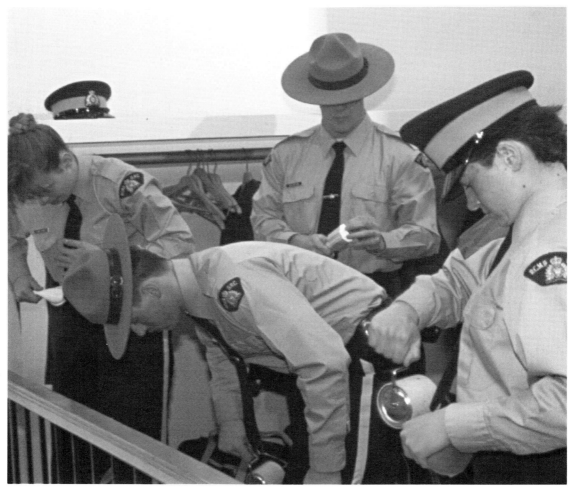

Recruits quickly learn to pay detailed attention to their uniforms. Suzanne Lund, Joe Kohut, Dave Attew and Kathy Furgason (l-r) remove lint with a tape roller.

Lund was intelligent, but she had just finished university and was only twenty-four years old. She wasn't keen on taking charge of a troop which consisted mostly of men, most of whom were older than she was. "I thought any day I'd walk into drill and I'd be off the hook," she recalled, "so I never really got organized or got into a system of managing the troop until I realized five weeks had gone by." By that time, Troop 17's unity had started to deteriorate, and rifts were developing in the group. Some of the men felt that Lund's appointment was a public relations effort to counter criticisms that women were being discriminated against by the force. Some believed it was part of a "head game" being played by Ferguson and the other instructors, an attempt to test the recruits and determine how much aggravation they could take without becoming upset. They theorized that the mostly-male troop was being put to some kind of test, to see how it would respond to the leadership of a young woman.

Suzanne Lund, right marker, inspects troop formation before drill class starts.
The right marker, the troop leader, is responsible for troop discipline.

~43~

When Lund began to realize that she was not going to be relieved of the right marker's responsibilities, she struggled to come to grips with the job, uncertain how much authority she had, and how much of that she should exert. Sometimes she did things that rubbed many of the men the wrong way. For instance, one day she decided that gun holsters were going to be worn outside the jackets. All the men in the troop had come out of their barracks and lined up ready to march to class with their holsters inside their jackets. That was a decision which they had made among themselves, and there was a lot of grumbling when they had to take off their jackets and do it Lund's way.

The men lived together in a building called D Block, while the women were in another building known as B Block. Inevitably, there were communications problems. Lund would make a decision, but she couldn't just tell everybody in the barracks to "listen up," as a male right marker would have done. Lund had to reach the men's barracks by phone, or she had to walk over to D Block and tell them in person. Sometimes, by the time she got her message across, some of the men had already left the barracks because they were in the band or had other duties.

Kathy Furgason makes last minute adjustments prior to Corporal Ferguson's arrival.

As the weeks rolled by, discontent over Lund's leadership began to build, and troop unity suffered. This was a serious problem, since much of their success depended on their ability to get along and work together. A happy, cohesive troop won the respect of the instructors, while a fragmented troop was viewed with contempt. The instructors said that if the recruits couldn't work together in training, maybe they would have trouble working with the people in their detachments. Failure to be a team player, failure to fit in with others in the RCMP, was seen as a major inadequacy. Troops which couldn't get their acts together were quickly labelled by their instructors as "shit troops," and that meant they got a hard time during training.

Lund knew that it was up to her to make sure her troop worked together, but she wasn't sure what to do. "I was making these decisions longer and longer. I was wondering when is this going to end, and some of the guys were wondering when is this going to end," she said later. "A couple of guys had a problem with the fact that I was a woman, or the fact that Pat lost it and I got it."

To make matters worse, some people in the troop found that Lund was a convenient focal point for their frustrations about life in general at the training academy. They couldn't go after the corporals or the higher-ups, but they could bellyache about Lund.

Their discontent took several forms. There was a lot of bitching behind Lund's back. Smart answers were sometimes given when she called the roll. People complained that she was not holding enough drill practices. Worst of all, there was sometimes talking in the ranks. This was strictly forbidden, and taken as a sign that a troop really lacked discipline and respect for the right marker.

"It was just getting to the point where there was a lot of pressure, and there were a couple of guys in the troop not willing to co-operate or put forth the effort," Lund said. "They were hostile in drill practices, or when I gave an order, they wouldn't co-operate, or they would make a snide comment before complying. I thought it was very immature, because I've never been unreasonable in asking people to do things."

But her friend and troopmate, Colette Perrier, said that Lund "kind of dug her own hole." When things were at their worst, just before the halfway point in training, Perrier felt that "it's at the point where I don't think a lot of the guys have any respect for her as right marker. They're not listening to her, and she can yell and scream and jump up and down and do what she wants, but she's lost it. She's beyond that point."

Lund started looking for a way out. She went to the troop's guidance counsellor, Corporal Dan Nugent, to talk about the possibility that she might resign as right marker. She didn't know if she could just walk away from it like that, but she had come to the conclusion that "the job sucks," and she would have happily given it up. But Nugent told her she had been given a job to do, and that she should do it. He told Lund that Mounties often have to do things they don't want to do, and she might as well get used to it while she was still in training.

So Lund finally decided that it was time to take charge. She called a meeting and told the troop that it looked like she was going to remain as the right marker, and they should try and make the best of it. She told them they were in an "us" against "them" situation, Troop 17 versus the Academy, and that they should work with her and work together to help each other get through.

Lund combined this friendly, reasonable approach with a bit of muscle. As the right marker, she had a fair amount of authority, and she began to assert some of it, while wisely holding back from using the ultimate power she had, which was to issue a "chit," a written reprimand which would go to the sergeant major and also onto the recruit's record at the Academy.

"You can't prevent people from feeling the way they feel," Lund concluded. "The only thing you can do is prevent them from voicing it in public. I took one guy aside and told him if I ever caught him saying anything like that in front of me again, I'd chit him myself and send him to the SM. I fined another guy five dollars. These things are very unnecessary. You don't say things in public around here, not when you're marching."

As right marker, Lund is the key member of the troop. The right marker comes to attention before the drill corporal.

Eventually things improved. Nugent quietly told one of the men in the troop, Don Davidson, to take on the role of "left marker," normally just an administrative job, but expanded in this case to meet the special needs of a mostly-male troop with a female right marker. Davidson informally took over some of the power of the right marker. For instance, he decided how the men would dress, and he would tell Lund what they were wearing on a given day. And it was usually Davidson, not Lund, who was in charge when the troop marched from class to class. Davidson commanded the respect of the men, and he wouldn't tolerate any talking in the ranks, so that problem came to an end.

Lund remained in the right marker job to the end of training, and while some men never accepted her as the troop's leader, they gradually gave up fighting it. As the end of training came into sight, even the most outspoken critics of Lund's leadership stopped complaining. They looked to Davidson for their direction, and told themselves that they would soon be leaving the Academy, and it wouldn't matter who had been right marker.

The corporal accepts the clip board and dismisses the right marker, who then returns to the troop. After roll call, the recruits are inspected. Those with faults are "chitted," a form which itemizes the offence and goes in the recruit's file. They later receive some type of "corrective training."

As training progresses drill staff start to lose their fierceness. It starts to become a game where each participant knows the rules. Corporal Bob Stewart replaced Corporal Ian Ferguson as drill instructor near the mid-point of training due to holiday scheduling.

"To the front, salute," barks Corporal Stewart and the troop in unison snaps a brisk salute.

The other two women in Troop 17, Colette Perrier and Kathy Furgason, had an easier time of it than Lund and Crow. They went through training without having special responsibilities placed on their shoulders, and they were both physically fit, so they had no trouble coping with the physical demands. Perrier and Furgason also fit in well with the male members of the troop. In many ways, they were just another couple of "the guys."

But that didn't mean their sex was forgotten. They were well aware they were very much in the minority, and they looked for ways to get along with their male colleagues. When women were first accepted into the Mounties, in the 1970s, they were trained in all-female troops. Gradually that changed, and by the time Troop 17 came along, "mixed troops" consisting of both male and female members were fairly common. But usually there was a better balance of the sexes. Having only four women (and then only three after Crow left) meant that the women were a small minority.

Perrier and Furgason were determined to show the men in Troop 17 and their instructors that they were just as good as the male recruits. They succeeded in winning the men's esteem by performing well. They also took pains to cultivate friendships with some of the men, while steering clear of romantic involvements.

A slight mistake is quickly discouraged through pushups.

Colette Perrier was twenty-four. A gregarious, attractive brunette with a bright smile, Perrier was by far the smallest person in the troop. She was just five foot two and weighed 120 pounds, but she was self-confident and assertive, and that made her seem bigger. This was not the first time she had been in a job which was usually male-dominated. When Perrier finished high school, she signed up for a "women in non-traditional work" program and became a cabinet maker. She worked at this for six years, "but it got to the point where I was thinking this is not what I want to do when I'm thirty-five years old."

She had a few reservations about joining the Mounties. One of them was whether she could fit into a male-dominated organization. "I still don't think women are totally accepted here," she said after she had been in training for about three months. "It doesn't bother me. There's nothing blatant. It's just an undercurrent, just feelings. There are no discriminatory remarks. It's just who I am, and my capabilities are under closer scrutiny. Having worked in a man's job before, I know all about that. I had to work five times harder than any guy to prove myself. It's the same here."

After her training started, Perrier was pleasantly surprised by the attitude of most of the men in Troop 17. "I think we've got one of the better troops. When we first got here, the women from other troops said, 'Oh ya, if those guys aren't chauvinist pigs now, they will be.' There seemed to be a big problem between the men and the women, but we tried to get this straightened out right from the beginning. I haven't seen any problems since. I get along with everybody in the men's dorm."

The three remaining female members of Troop 17, Kathy Furgason, Colette Perrier and Suzanne Lund.

Perrier had no trouble keeping clear of romantic entanglements. She was engaged to a man outside the force and was planning to marry him after she graduated. And there was an unwritten rule that recruits did not date other recruits in the same troop. Friendship and mutual support were highly prized, but crossing the line into romance was frowned upon, mainly because it was seen as potentially disruptive to troop unity.

Perrier's bubbly personality helped her make friends with some of the men in her troop. Sometimes she would go over to the men's barracks in the evening. "I try and make a point of going over there at least a couple of times in the week," she said, "It's not just the girls over here doing their own things together, and only seeing the guys during the day."

Perrier was raised in Regina, and she was the only "home-towner" in the troop. She had visited the training academy many times while she was growing up, and had always been drawn to the idea of joining the RCMP, but because the force had minimum physical size requirements, "I just put it out of my mind." Those requirement were dropped a few years earlier, but "I didn't realize that height and weight restrictions had been eliminated until a friend told me. I had been carrying around in my head the Hollywood stereotype of a Mountie."

She looked back on her own misconceptions and laughed. "The RCMP has changed a lot, and I'm a good example." Perrier had little use for traditionalists who felt that things had changed too much, and that letting a woman as small as she was into the force was a bad idea. She hotly disputed any suggestion that perhaps she was too tiny to handle the job.

"I got a lot of that before I got into the RCMP, but then I've had that all my life because I'm short. That stuff doesn't bother me. I know my capabilities and my limitations. Sure, I'm not going to take on some six-foot-seven, 250-pound person. I know that's beyond my limitations. But there's not too many people who look at a police officer in uniform and think they're going to take him on. I think there is still respect for someone who's in a uniform."

She said she had also learned a lot during her training about ways to handle people without getting physical with them. "The idea is not just to go out and get in fights. There's more to it than that. Sure, that is a possibility, but I know my limitations, and I'm not going to go in there and get myself killed. I'm not stupid." She said she would have a baton and a gun and would use them if she had to, but that being a good police officer had more to do with presence and confidence than with size and weaponry. "Someone might look at me and I'm small and everything, but I'm not backing away from him, so maybe he'll think twice. I'm not going in there and committing suicide, but I'm not running away with my tail between my legs either. I've got a mouth on me. I've got a brain."

Perrier had little trouble with the physical side of training. She was in good shape, with a lot of upper body strength from lifting sheets of plywood in her former job as a cabinet maker. She also jogged, swam and lifted weights before she started training. "I was in better shape than I thought I was. I've surprised myself with some of the things I've been able to do here."

Colette Perrier. "I still don't think women are totally accepted here. There's nothing blatant. It's just an undercurrent."

Colette Perrier mugs with Joe Kohut. "I think we've got one of the better troops going through here . . . I get along with everybody in the men's dorm."

When Perrier needed a partner in gym and self-defence class, she often teamed up with Kathy Furgason, who was also small, although at five foot three and 135 pounds she was a little bigger than Perrier. Furgason's short hair gave her a boyish look. She had a pixie-like grin, and always seemed to be smiling. Even more than Perrier, she seemed to fit into the troop as "one of the boys."

Furgason's male troopmates responded well to her upbeat personality, and they admired her spirit. They liked her positive attitude and the fact that she never complained. She just quietly got on with the job. Furgason, in turn, thought a lot of her male troopmates. "I really like every one of them."

She formed an especially close friendship with Kerry Mah, a Chinese-Canadian who had suffered a lot of discrimination, especially when he was younger. "I know what it's like to be at the bottom," said Mah, "and I know it hasn't been easy for the women. Kathy Furgason has proved a lot to me. She's in better shape than most of the guys and she's got a lot more spunk than just about anybody in the troop. But she's also got a soft side. She's the one that I lean on quite a bit, and she leans on me. I've never had a sister, but if I did, it's her. She's been there for me."

Colette Perrier and Suzanne Lund try to subdue Brian Davison during self-defence class.

~53~

Kathy Furgason and Kerry Mah formed an especially close friendship. "Kathy Furgason has proved a lot to me . . . she's got a lot more spunk to her than just about anybody in the troop." — Mah.

Furgason, like Perrier, felt some initial apprehension when she was put into a troop in which the men so heavily outnumbered the women. "When we first got into the troop, a lot of the guys didn't want us. They didn't want a co-ed troop," she remembered. But she found that the men soon came to respect her and Perrier because they were physically fit, and because they were not afraid of getting hurt in self-defence class. "I think they accept us because we don't back out like some of the girls in other troops might," Furgason said. "They respect us for doing everything they do."

Furgason was one of the youngest members of the troop. She was only twenty-one, and several of the men, like Mah, encouraged her to think of them as big brothers. Sometimes one of the men would give her a hand, and she knew how to accept it gracefully. "Dave Tyreman is a better runner than I am," she noted. "One day we were out running and he said, 'I'll stick with you all the way.' He ran with me, and he pushed me to do my best. He said, 'Okay, Fergie, make your strides bigger. You don't have to go fast. Just take bigger strides.'" And when the run was over, she thanked him for his help without giving him the impression that she was a little girl dealing with a big man.

Furgason came from Hamiota, a community of about 700 people in western Manitoba. She applied to the RCMP when she was about eighteen and passed the written test, but was turned down when eye examinations by two doctors showed that she was too near-sighted to meet the force's entrance requirements. But a recruiter told her mother that the force really needed women, and suggested that Kathy be retested. "They passed me," Furgason said. "I think it was just a different test that they had. They told me I even had room to spare." By the time she had completed all the steps involved in getting accepted, she was just a year short of a degree from the University of Winnipeg, with a double major in psychology and justice and law enforcement. She hoped to complete her degree someday.

Furgason was one of the few recruits in the troop who thoroughly enjoyed her training. While most of the others grumbled a lot, and grudgingly accepted the need to go through the Academy in order to become police officers, Furgason joked about getting paid to have so much fun at the Academy. "I actually love it here," she said when she was about half way through. "A lot of people say this is the worst place on earth, that it's like hell, but I really enjoy it here. Everything we get to do is so exciting! The driving, the shooting. People would die for chances like that."

Furgason had a remarkable ability to stay out of trouble. "I just blend in with thirty other people," she said. While many of her troopmates were frequently getting nailed for one thing or another, Furgason always seemed to do things right. She had never been "chitted" for doing something wrong, but once she was given a "positive chit" after she scored 100 percent on an exam in her human relations class. "But I think my time will come," she predicted. "They'll go back and check through the records and then, hey, I'll get toasted."

Her time finally came when she was in her second-last week of training. She was responsible for raising the flag in the morning, and somehow it managed to get upside down on the pole. Nobody noticed until mid-morning, and then there was a big uproar about it, and Furgason was blamed. She innocently said she must have made a mistake because it was so dark that early in the morning, but some people thought she did it on purpose, so she could say she didn't go through training without getting into trouble just once.

Kathy Furgason and Dave Rampersad on a run.

chapter three

"Discipline has to come from within."

When they needed advice or a shoulder to cry on, the recruits in Troop 17 turned to Dan Nugent. He was an instructor in the Academy's operational training unit, but he wasn't as hard-nosed as some of the others tended to be. Nugent had a relaxed attitude and a good sense of humor, and he helped the recruits see there was a fulfilling life waiting for them in the RCMP, if they could make it through the grind at the Academy.

Nugent wasn't one of their regular teachers. He was their guidance counsellor, and the assignment enabled him to deal with them on a less formal basis. He was friendly, but he was no bleeding heart. "I'm not going to put my fingers in your nostrils and drag you through this place," he told them. When they complained about their hard life, he told them it should be harder. He told them stories about all the Christmas Eves he'd had to work, and all the times he'd rattled doorknobs at 4 a.m. Nugent said if he was in charge, their training would be even more rigorous, because it would get them ready for the life of a working cop.

"I'd make it tougher because I think it's important that they learn how to discipline themselves here," he said. "When you're in the middle of nowhere in the middle of the night in the middle of a snowbank, just waiting for something to happen for ten or twelve or fifteen hours, discipline has to come from within."

Nugent was firm, but he cared about the recruits. He and his wife Thelma had the troop over to their house at Christmas, where the recruits marvelled at such things as a home-cooked meal and a warm, family-like atmosphere. It was a welcome change from the Spartan life they had been living at the Academy. Nugent remembered his own days as a recruit, and how different it was from civilian life.

Corporal Dan Nugent, Troop 17's Guidance NCO.

"I was sort of a child of the sixties with the long hair," he recalled. "I wore a beard for six or seven years before I entered the force." He shaved off his beard and cut his hair before arriving at the Academy in 1976. "I had my own way of looking at things. When I came here, I thought this place was absolutely nuts. My lifestyle until then had been much different, and the people I had associated with were not the usual RCMP types."

Nugent grew up on Cape Breton Island and studied arts at university for three years, then went to Montreal. He applied to the RCMP, but it took almost two years before he was accepted, and he enjoyed himself while he bided his time. "I was a young guy kicking around, sowing oats, whether they were wild or otherwise, working in a factory, working for a snow removal outfit and doing other things until I got in."

When he arrived in Regina, he didn't feel much like a member of the RCMP. He looked around in amazement at the uniforms, the marching, the regimentation. "I kind of got a kick out of it. It was quite funny in some respects. My first day here, some recruit was sitting on top of the airplane in front of the museum, polishing the thing. I thought this place was neat, different."

It didn't take him long to fit in. He did well in training, but like many recruits he had trouble in one particular area. Nugent's nemesis was driving. He thought it was going to be a breeze. "I thought I could drive anything," he remembered. "I kind of got hit in the face with the fact that I wasn't a very good driver. I was twenty-three years old, and I had prided myself on my ability to handle a motor vehicle. The motor skills were no problem. It was the

Arron Polk relaxes with Dan Nugent at Troop 17's "halfway" party.

~58~

concentration and observation skills that I lacked. I was on extra driving probably four of the six months I was here. Even now, when I walk past the post garage in the winter time, I just shudder when I see the clouds of exhaust smoke hanging in the air."

He was the first person in his troop to be sent to the sergeant major, after a senior recruit nailed him for not wearing a tie when he was in civilian dress in the mess hall. When Nugent stood at attention before the SM, "the sergeant screamed blue bloody murder. Oh, what a horrible person I was to dare to walk into the division mess without a tie on. How could I ever discipline myself to be an effective policeman? How he made some of the connections, I don't know."

Nugent came to think of the Academy as a fantasy world. "I can remember getting off the plane when I arrived, and a recruit who was at the airport said, 'Welcome to Disneyland.' There's an element of being removed from the world here. It's a self-contained and enclosed sort of system. The regimentation, the adherence to a strict code of discipline, constantly being called by my rank, that sort of thing is not a reproduction of the real world. I would be quite embarrassed to be called 'corporal' by any constable in most situations, unless it's a very formal thing, in court or something like that. But the things that happen here are necessary. The devices that we set up in training have to be unreal, because the recruits have to be doing things that can be controlled, that they can succeed at in a brief period of time. An actual investigation can go on for months. I set one up here, and it's going to be cleared up in an hour and a half. There's a self-contained, insulated quality about this place."

Nugent spent his first year after training in Ottawa, patrolling embassies and escorting VIPs. He was a bodyguard for Prime Minister Pierre Trudeau's children. Then he went to his first detachment, which was in Labrador City, where he spent three years. After that he worked in other places in Newfoundland, moving every few years and gaining experience in new areas. He passed on his enthusiasm for routine policing to the recruits. "I just love it. I get a kick out of it. I'm even more enthusiastic than when I started fourteen years ago. I like the interaction, meeting people, scooting out of the detachment, making those police cars go as fast as you can, dealing with all kinds of emergency, the day-to-day stuff, banging on doors and dealing with kids."

But while he was working in the field, he started thinking about returning to the Academy as an instructor. It's a common ambition. Many who go through the place as recruits dream of coming back as instructors. "I never saw myself as a school teacher as such," said Nugent, "but I think back to my own instructors. They had a lot of experience which they were able to pass on, and they were pretty good role models. That's what I try to be."

Dr. Bob Roy got to keep his beard when he joined the Mounties, and didn't have to go through recruit training, but he was no bleeding heart either. Roy was the Academy's psychologist. A warm, relaxed man, he liked to joke about being a "shrink" and a "mind

~59~

expander" and compare himself to a university guidance counsellor, but he didn't think the Academy should try to serve everybody. A lot of people just aren't meant to be Mounties, he said, and the Academy was a place where they could get a good taste of the RCMP before committing themselves to a career in the force.

"The average university student changes four and a half times in his career track, trying to find his niche," Roy pointed out. "The same applies here. Despite everything they may have heard or read about the RCMP, some recruits have doubts, or they have decided they don't want to be here. Then it becomes a question of how do you leave and save face. What are you going to say to all of your relatives, particularly to Uncle Joe, who is a former superintendent in the force."

People also come to Roy for help in coping with the Academy's high stress level and heavy workload. He doesn't hold their hand and tell them they are treated badly. Rather, he encourages them to manage their time better, so they can do everything that is expected of them. He tells them that "this is a preview of what awaits you out there. There are not that many occupations that allow you this kind of a preview. This is a golden opportunity to find out within the space of six months whether this is something you're going to like."

He explains the Academy intentionally puts a lot of pressure on the recruits so those not suited to be Mounties can be weeded out. "If you can survive the training academy, you can probably survive front-line policing. The six months at the Academy is very intense. It stands for at least a good year of university anywhere, in my opinion. It's go, go, go, morning, noon and night. You don't have study breaks and things like that. It is intense, high speed, continuous. If you can manage that and stay in shape and come out of it relatively unscathed, you've got a good chance. We make no apologies for it. If you want us to tone down the stress level, then you should start wondering whether you should be here in the first place."

Roy said recruits suffering from stress-related problems frequently don't express it in those terms. They complain about being tired all the time, or about having insomnia, or feeling grouchy and moody. Roy often found that these were symptoms of other problems, and he would try to help them "get in touch with reality" and find out what was really bothering them. Identifying the real problem was the first step to overcoming it.

Sometimes the recruits were just bothered by isolation and homesickness. "It's hard to keep your mind on an exam here when your wife is about to have a baby in Quebec City or British Columbia. It's hard to feel like you're being a good family man when your wife has her hands full with two pre-schoolers."

Joking helps the recruits relieve their stress. Often the jokes are sexual in nature. The men complain about having to live in single-sex dorms and say that "it's hard to sleep with a flagpole between your legs." Roy said this sort of "beer parlor humor is common, especially among young males. I don't think it's unique to the Academy. Certainly joking is done a lot in the RCMP, not only in the Academy. I think every profession has its own type of jokes, which outside of that profession will look a little black or out of context or off color, but within the profession we know it is there to release tension."

Having to live in a regimented environment and in close quarters in the barracks was hard on the men, but Roy said it imposed even more stress on the women. "On average, the men handle it much better than the women. To come to the Academy and have your hair cut, to get into the same type of uniform, to live in close quarters without any privacy, is much harder for a woman, and yet they manage after awhile."

Roy said that out of a typical troop, two or three recruits usually paid him a visit. Patient-doctor confidentiality prevented him from talking about individual cases, but at least one member of Troop 17 consulted the psychologist, and eventually became the second member of the troop to leave.

❖   ❖   ❖

"I was over to see Dr. Roy three times," said Len Peters, "including the morning I left. He was quite helpful." It was a Friday, the end of the troop's fourteenth week of training, with just ten more weeks to go. While his troopmates were in a classroom filling out forms which indicated their preferred first postings, Peters was in the administration building signing another form which ended his career in the Mounties.

Peters had a lot of trouble with the physical aspects of training, but his downfall was aquaphobia. He couldn't handle the swimming program. Ten other members of the troop were also non-swimmers or could swim only a few strokes when they arrived, but they all managed to learn to swim well enough to pass their tests. None of them carried the additional burden of being afraid of the water. It was a problem that had plagued Peters all his life, and at times it was so bad he would start to tremble in the class before Troop 17 was scheduled to go to the pool.

"The water is a foreign environment to me," Peters observed. "I've taken lessons in the past but it just didn't seem that I progressed very much. I really don't know how to explain it. I get in the water and I seize up and I can't seem to do anything." He tried his best, swimming three nights a week for extra practice despite his intense dislike of the water. He felt that with more time and extra help from the instructors, he might have been able to pass the tests which required him to swim several lengths of the pool and be able to rescue someone who was drowning.

In one class, when an instructor was able to spend a whole period with Peters, he managed to swim a couple of lengths on his back. But another time, he recalled, "I had to be rescued, and that did a whole lot for my confidence. I tried to tread water in the seven-foot end and I went under about three times and I lost control, so a guy had to jump in and pull me to the side. It was a big step backwards."

Peters was called into the standards office to discuss his lack of progress in swimming, and eventually advise that he should consider resigning. "They told me they didn't have the time, nor did they have the resources, to help me with this problem," Peters said. "I would have to seek assistance outside the force. I was told that if I decided to stay, they were going to do a medical evaluation and recommend discharge for psychological reasons." Peters wasn't happy about that. "Actually, I thought it was pretty shitty, to be quite honest with you. I guess they had justification, but initially I didn't feel I was doing that badly, and I felt I could meet the base standard at the end of the swimming program. They didn't agree with me."

Peters felt that he should have received special instruction right from the start, rather than being expected to do what all the others in the troop did. His fear of the water was identified in the first class. "It brings into question the training practices," he said. "I wasn't going to get into a big argument with them over their technique, because obviously it works more times than it doesn't work, so who the hell am I to second-guess their training methods? But I just felt if I could learn to swim on my back in forty-five minutes with one instructor, then why couldn't I do that before I'd already gone through fourteen hours of classes?"

Peters was married and had two children. At thirty-three, he was the second-oldest member of the troop, but he might have been able to lick his swimming difficulty if he hadn't also had a lot of other physical problems. "When I first got there," he recalled, "I partially separated my right shoulder. I bruised my rib, I buggered my knees up, I had a sore back, and I jammed my big toe on my left foot when I was sparring." He fell behind his troopmates in self-defence class, and the instructor told the standards office he didn't think Peters was going to pass one of his key exams, which involved wrestling vigorously with an opponent.

Len Peters finishes a set of situps while troopmates jog by. Peters, at 33 the second oldest member of the troop, had trouble with the physical aspects of training.

"I knew him pretty well," said Dave Attew, after Peters left. "He was the type of person everyone could like, but he just didn't fit in. It wasn't just the swimming. It was his whole body. He was at the age where everything was hurting. He wasn't a young man and he didn't have the physical abilities to do a lot of the stuff. Add on the fact that he was scared of the water."

When he started having real trouble, Peters thought he might be backtrooped. He went home to Drumheller, Alberta, for the weekend to talk things over with his wife, but then he ran into further difficulties. "I was sick with the cold and the flu all that weekend. I got back to the Academy Sunday night and I ended up in the medical treatment centre for three days. Well, the second day I'm there, the staff sergeant from standards comes up and more or less accuses me of being a gold-bricker, all this kind of nonsense, because I'm in the medical treatment centre with a cold and the flu. He said enough's enough, and we're going to do this medical evaluation, so I just decided I would resign."

Peters said he was told that if he left the Academy on his own accord, he would be able to reapply if he managed to get his aquaphobia under control. "I also didn't want it to show on my work file that I had been discharged by the RCMP for psychological reasons. I'm not a nut bar or anything like that."

Peters had always wanted to be a policeman. "I had applied before, when I was nineteen, and was unsuccessful. I just put it on the back burner and got a job working as a prison guard, and I did that for ten and a half years. I decided one day I'd give it another try. They were still doing priority hiring of women and visible minorities, but they took my application anyway and said we might be in touch, and lo and behold, one day I got a letter saying they were ready to proceed with my application, and two years later I was in."

On his last day at the Academy, he turned in his gun, his uniform and everything else he had been issued, signed his release papers, and after a few hurried farewells from his troopmates, he drove out the gate. He was angry and hurt, but in the end, "I decided to just chalk it up to experience. My options are all open. I can do just about whatever I want now. My mother told me when I came home, 'This is the first bad thing that's ever happened to you in your life. Things have been going along pretty good for you for the last thirty-odd years.' I had to agree with her. I haven't really had a whole lot to complain about. I gave it my best shot. I'm not going to hang my head in shame or anything."

Yvon Mercier, like Len Peters, had painful memories of the Academy's swimming pool. One day when Mercier was a twenty-year-old recruit, an instructor almost drowned him. "I was a fair swimmer before I came here," he recalled. "I could survive. I could save my own life. But the instructor, it seemed to me, didn't care. He just pushed me in and went under with me, and he made sure I had the scare of my life. Trainees, or at least those who are non-swimmers, will tell you today that swimming is a nightmare, but we now have much easier training methods for beginners. The instructors then came from what we now call the old school, and all of them were harsh on the recruits."

That was back in 1970. By the time Troop 17 came through the Academy, Mercier had risen to the rank of sergeant major. A robust-looking, self-confident man, balding and greying on the temples, the SM, as everyone called him, was in charge of "deportment," a broad term covering everything from the way the recruits wore their uniforms to the way they acted in class and conducted themselves outside training. When they got into trouble, they were ordered to "have tea with the SM," which meant reporting to his office and standing at attention in front of his desk. "Sometimes," he said, "they are shaking in their boots."

The sergeant major had little time for excuses or explanations. "I'm very square and plain with them. There's never a good reason for being untidy or scruffy on parade. When you're given instructions, comply with them. It's pretty straightforward."

Practising for the swimming final. "We now have much easier training methods for beginners." —Mercier

The corrective training dispensed by the SM was usually confinement to the barracks for the weekend, and perhaps also writing a 500-word essay. Mercier said the loss of freedom was painful to many recruits, who would rather be home with their families or out drinking with their pals than stuck on the base and reporting every hour to the guard room. But for all his insistence that corrective training was necessary, Mercier sometimes gave recruits a break. For instance, if they already had a non-refundable plane ticket home for the weekend, he'd let them serve their confinement to the barracks the following weekend.

He said recruits were sometimes afraid of him, but they also knew the system was just. "If they screw up, they're going to pay for it. They appreciate the fairness and the way the system treats them." He said they knew they could undergo their corrective training and that would be that. Dealing with the standards office was more frightening, because it could lead to resignation or discharge proceedings.

Mercier said the Academy's instructional methods had improved a lot since the days when he went into the pool with the instructor who almost drowned him. "I firmly believe that we are preparing trainees to take on their first tasks in the field 200, 300 percent better than when I joined the force." He said one improvement was that "we had to learn everything the hard way. The instructor would come in and say, 'I want this dorm to be spic and span and spotless,' without giving any instructions. Now everything is structured, and we go step by step explaining to them what is required."

Mark Davidson in the pool. Swimming class took its toll on the recruits. Some recruits came to the Academy unable to swim. "Trainees, at least those who are non-swimmers, will tell you today that swimming is a nightmare." — Mercier.

When Mercier arrived, he didn't speak English, but as far as the Academy was concerned, that was his problem. He didn't receive any language training, as recruits do now, and classes weren't offered in French, as they are today. "Not only did I have to keep up with the classes, but all of it was taught in my second language, and I could barely say yes or no at that time, so there was a lot to be learned. Needless to say, I was kind of lost for the first couple of months, but then learning under pressure I found was the answer. I learned quickly, and I coped with the various parts of the training after my second month, but I must admit that the first two months were very difficult."

Another big change had come in the area of discipline. When Mercier was a recruit, "it was harsh. Now we try to avoid the word discipline. We refer to it as corrective training. Then, it was discipline. All instructional staff were to ensure that discipline was the main topic." For example, recruits in 1970 often had to "stand-to," which meant they had to stand by their bed in their best uniforms and be inspected by the duty NCO several nights in a row. "Stand-tos were not only to punish, but to cause a lot of inconvenience to the trainees who had misplaced some part of their kit or their kit was not up to snuff," Mercier recalled. "That was given to us perhaps two or three times a month. Like the recruits do now, we felt the

An eight-second time exposure of Troop 17 during the stand-to. Any movement by a recruit would blur the image.

~66~

dorms were in good shape, but there was always some little thing that would cause a stand-to. We still have stand-tos today, but they are oriented toward corrective training, and we teach the recruits how to prepare their dormitories, how to place the uniforms, and when they are found to be untidy they will usually get a stand-to, but it will be perhaps once or twice in their training period. We feel they get the message quickly, and when they have that message, we tend to leave it alone."

✣ ✣ ✣

It's 7:15 on a Friday night. The men of Troop 17 are lounging around in their barracks, some in half-uniform or civvies, others still in their underwear. They're tired after a rough week of training, but they're not finished yet. Their dorm was inspected the previous Monday, and some of their sleeping areas were found to be dirty, while others had items of clothing out of place or other things wrong. The sergeant major has ordered a stand-to for the whole troop.

Mark Davidson laces his boots in preparation for inspection. Although there is tension in the air, preparations are remarkably relaxed.

As the clock moves toward eight, the recruits explode in a burst of housekeeping, vacuuming, picking up and straightening, followed by a flurry of dressing and primping and preening. In a few minutes, they'll be required to stand at the foot of their beds, in full uniform. A corporal will inspect them, looking for the minutest flaws in their personal appearance and the condition of their living quarters.

The Academy has a fetish for neatness. There are hundreds of things which must be done just right, and the recruits never know when they'll be inspected, or what might be picked out for special attention. Troop 17 isn't sure what to expect tonight. The corporal who's coming, Wayne Plimmer, is unknown to them. He works in the Academy's administration office, and has drawn the Friday night shift as duty NCO. Right now he's in Troop 18's dorm, on the opposite side of D block. The members of Troop 17 can look across the courtyard and see Plimmer going down the line in Troop 18's quarters. Their dorm is next.

Everything is subject to inspection — every part of the recruits' uniforms, every item of their kit, every square inch of their living space. The recruits joke that there are three ways to do everything — the right way, the wrong way, and the RCMP way. Many feel the RCMP way sometimes doesn't make a lot of sense. Why, for instance, would anyone in his right mind get excited about a tiny speck of lint on the edge of a blanket? Why lace up your shoes before you put them in the closet when you've just got to unlace them again to put them on?

But recruits don't have a say in such matters, and now that they're well into their training, the members of Troop 17 have learned to just go with the flow and do what they're told. They seem more like brow-beaten high school kids than men. Most adopt the attitude that the RCMP's training methods have stood the test of time, and if they don't always make perfect sense, they work. The important thing is to do whatever it takes to make Plimmer happy tonight, and get on with life. Soon they'll be out of the Academy, but right now they're just thinking about getting out of the barracks tonight.

But they've been around long enough to know how the game works. If Plimmer is inclined to be tough, pouncing on them for the slightest imperfection, they'll surely fail the inspection the first time around. Some of the recruits speculate that no matter how perfect they are, the corporal will be impossible to please. They wonder whether he has been ordered to fail them the first time. If they don't pass the eight-o'clock inspection, they'll have to go through the whole thing again a couple of hours later, and if they fail that one, they'll have to do it over the next morning.

Stand-tos, like a lot of other things at the Academy, go back to the beginning of RCMP recruit training in the nineteenth century. There used to be stand-tos every week. The commanding officer, the training officer, the sergeant major and the division orderly would go through each barracks every Saturday morning, and the recruits couldn't go downtown to drink beer until they had passed muster. But over the decades, the importance of stand-tos gradually decreased. This is Troop 17's second and last stand-to.

They had their first one before Christmas. That night, the NCO in charge of the Academy's firearms section, Staff Sergeant Gary Faulconbridge, happened to be the duty

NCO. Naturally, he checked their service revolvers. Some of them were dirty, and Faulconbridge ordered the whole troop to stand-to again the following morning.

The Academy justifies stand-tos on the grounds that the recruits learn to pay attention to detail. A recruit who manages to pay attention to every detail in preparation for a stand-to inspection supposedly can employ the same skill when he's at the scene of a crime. Stand-tos are also said to instil the concept of collective responsibility. The RCMP puts a lot of emphasis on teamwork. And having to stand-to because of the shortcomings of others in the troop is seen as preparation for a life which is sometimes unfair. If you can grit your teeth and bear a stand-to, even if you personally did nothing wrong, you can do the same when you feel like wringing the neck of a citizen who lays an unfounded complaint against you.

Stand-tos are also supposed to engender an esprit de corps, a sense of pride and solidarity that comes from sharing common experiences, particularly under adversity. The idea is that tonight's stand-to will provide the recruits with pleasant memories, one more hardship to savor in retrospect. But that lies well ahead. Tonight most members of Troop 17 are not pleased about being cooped up in their dorm. There are plenty of other things they'd rather be doing on a Friday evening. Lorin Lopetinsky is typical. He can hardly wait to get this

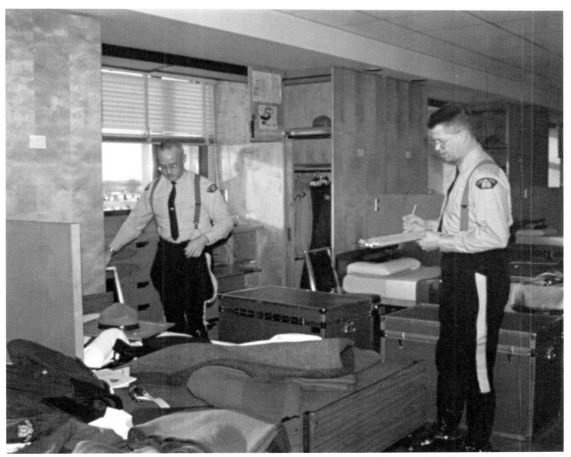

Corporals Bob Stewart and Ian Ferguson inspect Troop 17's dorm. The two go carefully through each recruit's living area and throw anything not up to standards onto the recruit's bed. By the end of inspection it is understandable why the recruits refer to it as "trashing the dorm."

nonsense over. He's got a date at nine o'clock; he knows that if the troop fails the first time around, he'll miss it.

The recruits see the stand-to as punishment, but the Academy says it's corrective training decreed after the surprise dorm inspection the previous Monday morning. Troop 17 had already been hit once before, in early December, when the recruits were about two months into their training. Corporal Ferguson, who jokingly called himself "The Phantom of the Dorm," turned up one day and tore the place apart. He kept up a running monologue as he went from pit to pit. "MacKay, you piggie, you!" he exclaimed when he found dirt in Trevor MacKay's cupboard, tossing items from the cupboard onto the bed and floor. When he spotted a dead fly in the corner of another recruit's closet, he solemnly noted the offence and pronounced that "pets are not allowed." He pulled unfastened raincoats from their hangers and threw them on the floor.

Corporal Ian Ferguson, the "Phantom of the Dorm," checks for dust by using a recruit's hat as a duster.

Ferguson was jubilant when he discovered a key at the bottom of a cupful of pens and pencils. The key fit Dan Thorne's storage trunk, which was supposed to be "secured at all times." Ferguson opened the trunk and found cash, cassette tapes and a bag of dirty laundry. He considered dumping the contents of the trunk all over the floor, but settled for merely tossing the laundry onto the floor. Ferguson and his equally cheerful colleague, Corporal Bob Stewart, were at it again the previous Monday, once more striking when the recruits were in class. They found dust in the corners of several of the recruits' cupboards. They were just specks of dirt, but the corporals promptly magnified them into "dust elephants." Stewart joked that there was so much sand in one recruit's cupboard that it must be part of the set for *Lawrence of Arabia*. When the corporals found shirts with buttons undone, they cackled and tossed them onto the recruits' beds. Boots with less than a perfect gleam on their toes were hurled on the floor. The corporals struck pay dirt when they found Dave Rampersad's trunk unlocked, and made lewd remarks about the pinup pictures they found inside.

The corporals methodically made the rounds, turning the dorm into a shambles. It took them better than an hour, and while they joked around a lot, they were serious about their work and viewed it as an important part of training. They solemnly referred to it as a "barracks inspection," but the recruits called it "trashing the dorm," and viewed it as part of the game.

Corporals Stewart and Ferguson discover Dave Rampersad's trunk unlocked. The recruit's trunk is his private locker, the only place where he can store non-regulation items including valuables. If the Corporal can get into it, so, presumably, could anyone else. This means the recruit is guilty of failing to secure his valuables, a serious offense for which corrective training is required.

As the clock approaches eight, the recruits stand by their beds and joke around. They kid Rampersad about leaving his trunk lid up so his girlie pictures will be on display. Mark Gagnier strolls around urging his pals to "dimple" their pillows — poke an index finger into the corners — to give them that finished look. Then the three female members of the troop come in. Their dorm, in nearby B Block, will be inspected later, but they are required to stand-to with the men of the troop.

Plimmer arrives and right marker Suzanne Lund orders them to stand at attention. Plimmer begins making his rounds, and the room is silent. He takes a hat from its place on one recruit's bed and runs it, brim-side down, around the bottom of one of the cupboards. The dark blue felt material acts like a magnet, picking up bits of dirt and displaying them on the top of the hat. Plimmer shakes his head in disgust and puts a mark against the offending recruit's name on the clipboard he's carrying. He goes down the line, randomly running hats around inside cupboards, pulling jackets from their hangers and tossing them on beds. The minutes tick by and the room remains silent except for the sound of Plimmer's movements.

The recruits remain at attention, looking straight ahead, but every once in awhile one of them sneaks a peek to see what Plimmer is doing. When he's about thirty feet away, a couple of them indulge in some stealthy insubordination. They wink at each other and roll their eyes, trying to make the other one laugh. But their little game comes to an abrupt end when the heavy dorm door opens and a member of the senior troop enters. He's been assigned to work with Plimmer tonight, and he joins in the inspection.

The minutes drag by, and sounds from the newcomer's portable police radio break the silence every once in awhile. When that happens, the two rebellious recruits take advantage of the noise to have a quick conversation. One threatens to take the other's spurs off when the corporal leaves the dorm to check the washroom. But that idea dies when another member of the senior troop comes into the dorm. He stands watch while the corporal and his helper check the washroom, so there's no chance for tomfoolery.

The inspection takes about forty minutes. When it's over, Plimmer gives Lund a sheet of paper itemizing what he found wrong with each recruit's place. He leaves. A dour-faced Lund tells the recruits clustered around her that they have failed, and must stand-to again at 10:30. They groan at the unwelcome but not unexpected news. Lund tells them that the most common problem noted by Plimmer was that they did not have their patrol jacket zippers properly done up. The corporal said zippers were supposed to be pulled up only as far as the breast pockets. Many of the recruits had their jacket zippers done all the way up to the top, and others had left their jackets open.

There is general grumbling from the troop. Several of them say it is unfair, that they were previously told that the zippers were supposed to be pulled all the way to the top. Lund says she raised that point with Plimmer, but *he* said they should be only breast-high, so they failed. End of discussion. Lopetinsky, the recruit with the date at nine o'clock, is upset. His face twists, he swears, and he storms down the aisle toward his bed. A few others are also angry, but wiser heads tell them to shut up and cool it. It's all part of the game, a test to see how they react to disappointment. The hotheads mellow out. The recruits relax for a few minutes, then correct the things that Plimmer said were wrong and spend the rest of the time doing homework or polishing boots. They make sure their patrol jacket zippers are in the right place.

When Plimmer comes again at 10:30, he takes only about twenty minutes to make the rounds. Then he announces that they've passed the inspection. He drops his hard-nose act and tells them they've improved a lot. He suggests the recruits go out for a beer to celebrate. Five minutes later, Troop 17's dorm is empty.

Disappointment is evident on Dave Attew's face when they get the news they have failed their first dorm inspection. They will have to do a repeat performance later that night.

chapter four

"Welcome to hell."

Pat Zunti celebrated his thirty-fourth birthday while he was in training, but he felt he was being treated like a kid. "I've made my own decisions for a lot of years," he complained. "I've done things the way I wanted, and now all of a sudden I don't make my decisions. They decide when I eat, when I sleep, when I go to the can."

It was a lot like being a teenager again. On exams, Zunti had to feedback the answers the instructors wanted, no matter what he thought was right. He had to eat whatever food was dished up in the cafeteria, and when the gym teacher told him to run, he had to run whether he felt like it or not. When he was a bad boy, he had to see the sergeant major, who was like a cranky vice-principal handing out detentions.

Zunti scored in the nineties on his exams and was eager to learn, but he was expected to do a lot more than master the mechanics of policing. The Academy seemed to be trying to run his whole life and to completely make him over. He didn't think they would get very far. "I know who I am and what I am," he said. "I know what I can do and what I can't do, and I don't have to prove anything to anybody anymore."

He felt like he was moving down an assembly line, along with all the other trainees going through the big Mountie factory. They were processed from the time they woke up until the time they went to sleep, and five days a week was not enough to transform them into the finished products the force wanted. Even their weekends were not their own. Zunti had a wife and two little boys, but for the first three months of his training he was permitted to go home only one weekend a month. After that, he could leave the Academy every weekend, but only if he had no extra duties, and only if he had not been confined to the base for one reason or another.

That happened one weekend in February, after Zunti had been in training for about four months. He had worked hard so he could get away after classes on Friday afternoon. His six-year-old son missed his dad so much that he cried every time Zunti phoned home, and his wife Bev had her hands full with that boy and another one who was only two years old. Zunti was eager to be at home. He liked to tuck them in at night, but he was stuck in the dorm on that Friday night. The whole troop had to stay in because some of the recruits hadn't finished their first-aid homework. Zunti had his done, but that didn't matter. He was cooped up with the rest of them, like a teenager suffering through a class detention because other kids had misbehaved. Zunti felt it was unfair.

Another time he acknowledged he was in the wrong, but questioned the punishment he received. He had a few coins in his pocket, and when a corporal heard it jingle, he nailed

Zunti for "poor turnout." The penalty was a week of "bozo parade." He had to report at 7:40 each morning to the drill hall, where he was given a cursory inspection and dismissed just in time to rush to his first class at eight o'clock. Zunti thought it would have made more sense to simply tell him he shouldn't carry change in his pocket. He could have used the time in the morning to prepare for class.

It irked him that the Academy insisted on treating him like a juvenile delinquent who had to be slapped every time he strayed from the acceptable path. He thought the "corrective training" concept was childish, and said that no matter what name it was given, punishment was still punishment. Zunti was mad about a lot of things that went on during his training, but there was nothing he could do about it. If he wanted to graduate he had to go along with everything that was demanded of him. It had been made clear at the beginning that everyone would be treated the same way, and he didn't expect one set of rules for himself and another for the twenty-one-year-olds. He reconciled himself to the idea that it was best to just "go with the flow" and count the days until he would get out of there.

Pat Zunti, the oldest member of Troop 17, was elected to be the right marker. He directs the group between classes during orientation. Zunti, a former grain farmer, decided to try the RCMP when the prairie farming economy sputtered.

The system used to train Zunti and the others in Troop 17 went back to the nineteenth century, when the force was established. It modelled its ways after the British army. The idea was to keep a tight rein on the recruits initially, and eventually teach them to discipline themselves. This worked well at the beginning. Many of those who signed up were spirited and rebellious souls who had to be quickly transformed into sober and responsible men ready to take on the challenge of policing the Canadian frontier.

The emphasis on control and discipline continued into the twentieth century, when many recruits entered the force with only a Grade 8 education. The typical trainee was a boy from a farm or a small town who needed a firm hand and a lot of direction. The instructors used to say they were trying to put forty-year-old heads on twenty-year-old shoulders. The strategy was to knock the cockiness out of them and build them into Mounties from the ground up. Making them deal with horses was found to be particularly effective. Recruits were required to wash horses and clean up their messes, while their instructors talked about the outside of a horse being good for the inside of a man. They were thrown off the horses' backs and made to climb back on and stay on them until their backsides were raw. Sometimes they were even forced to wallow in manure and bathe in the horse troughs as punishment for minor infractions.

That kind of thinking had been officially abandoned a long time ago, and by the time Troop 17 came along the force recognized that it was no longer dealing with a bunch of farm boys, and that "negative motivators" weren't always the most conducive to learning. By the early 1990s, so many people with university degrees were applying that the force no longer gave them preferential treatment when considering their qualifications. Times had changed, recruits had changed, and Zunti thought it was time the Academy changed. The average age of the recruits in Troop 17 was twenty-five. About a quarter of them were married, and several more were planning to wed right after training. Most had been to college or university, or had held jobs for several years before coming to the Academy. The troop included people who had been teachers, computer experts, probation officers, accountants, mechanics and lab workers. Several had worked as security guards or served in the RCMP auxiliary before coming to the Academy.

Maturity and life experience were important considerations when their applications were considered, and it seemed strange to Zunti that the people selected should be treated like potential juvenile delinquents. Several people in Troop 17 had been turned down when they first applied to join the force. They were told they were too young, and advised to try again when they were older and had proven that they were responsible adults. But when they finally got to that point and made it into the Academy, it seemed as if the clock had been turned back. They felt they were treated like kids who couldn't be trusted and who were too stupid to make even the smallest decisions on their own.

The people in charge of training justified their methods by saying that the Academy always starts off by tightly controlling the lives of recruits, but gradually eases back as the recruits learn to accept responsibilities. They said they had been using the same basic technique for decades, and the methods had proven their worth. Besides, they said, they didn't do the things they did to make the recruits happy, but rather to make them good police officers. These were not students who were paying the RCMP for an education. They were employees who were being paid quite well to learn how to be useful members of the force, and this was the way the force had found worked best.

Zunti was typical of the increasing number of older recruits going through training at the Academy. He got into the Mounties after he had tried his hand at other things.

Zunti grew up in rural Saskatchewan. His grandfather emigrated from Switzerland, and his father ran a mixed cattle and grain farm near Unity, about 150 kilometres east of Saskatoon. After high school, he studied agriculture at the University of Saskatchewan for a couple years and then took over the family farm. Things went well at the beginning, but the prairie agricultural economy turned sour in the early 1980s. "The price of wheat went from $6 a bushel down to about $3. I was just starting out, and I couldn't survive." He and his wife Bev decided to get out of farming before they lost everything. "Both of us love the farm and the way of life, but we had to feed our family."

As a troop becomes more senior, they graduate from being part of the morning parade to supplying troop commanders for more junior troops. Troop commanders arrive early and await the arrival of their troops.

Mark Davidson and the other troop commanders await Corporal Ian Ferguson's inspection.

Corporal Ferguson inspects troop commanders Dave Attew and Mark Davidson. At this late stage of their training, criticism is more casual. Recruits are more likely to be reduced by Ferguson's wit than his wrath.

John Christensen leads his troop through its paces as the final stage of morning parade begins.

Zunti thought about joining the RCMP. He hoped it would provide him with a steady, well-paying job, but a recruiter told him there was no sense putting in an application because he couldn't speak French, didn't have a university degree, and wasn't female. Those were the force's "target groups" at the time, and people without at least one of those qualifications stood little chance of being hired. "I didn't have a hope of getting in," he concluded, "so I looked for something else." He tried selling insurance, but he didn't like it. He worked as an apprentice electrician, but kept getting laid off because the Saskatchewan economy was on the skids. "I had a couple of boys and a wife to support, and I needed something better, so I decided to apply to the RCMP anyway. I figured it couldn't hurt." That was in 1988. He got a phone call a year later. Like many others in Troop 17, Zunti benefitted from a change in force policy which broadened the selection criteria. Bilingualism and a university degree were still advantageous, but under the new policy applications from people lacking those qualifications were now considered.

The force had far more applications than it had places to fill. The pay and benefits were good. A constable could look forward to making about $47 000 a year plus overtime after just four years' service, and he could retire on a partial pension after just twenty years. The basic qualifications for getting into the force were not high, and Zunti met them all. An applicant had to be a Canadian citizen at least eighteen years of age, with a minimum of a high school education. He had to speak either English or French. He had to have a driver's licence. He needed good eyesight and had to be in good health and of "good character."

Zunti wrote two entrance exams, one covering subjects like social studies, math and English, the other to measure his intelligence and ability to learn. Then he filled out a medical questionnaire and a mountain of "suitability and security documents." These included the names and addresses of all his relatives, his work history for the past ten years, and many other things. Investigators went over everything, checking out his friends, relatives, neighbors and ex-employers, looking for what the Mounties term "areas of concern."

This includes such things as whether he had been affiliated with radical groups or suspected of criminal activity. His relatives were screened to see if he might have an uncle in prison, and his life was examined to see if he was the right sort of person to be a police officer, and whether he might have hidden something which would make him subject to blackmail.

He had to go through a three-hour interview. "They asked me everything, from whether I was gay to whether I was kinky to whether I could shoot somebody, and what I thought a policeman was or should be, and whether I did drugs. Everything I had ever done in my life was scrutinized, every bit of schooling, every employer."

At times, Zunti was frustrated by the Academy's insistence on treating him like a teenager. "I know who I am and what I am. I know what I can do and what I can't do, and I don't have to prove anything to anybody anymore."

Zunti came up almost clean. "The one thing that bothered them was that I had quite a few speeding tickets," Zunti said. "I had a heavy foot as a kid, and they didn't like that at all." But he hadn't had a ticket for a couple of years, and he said he had learned how to keep an eye on the speedometer. He underwent physical and dental examinations, and finally he was put on a waiting list, which meant he was just one step away from getting in.

"I was at the point in my life where I couldn't wait around for next year or the year after that. There are some fellows in our troop who have waited eight or ten years to get in here. I waited a year and a half, and I didn't have a lot more years to wait. When you get to my age, you have to start getting into something pretty secure. I was looking at applying to some of the city police forces, or possibly going back to school."

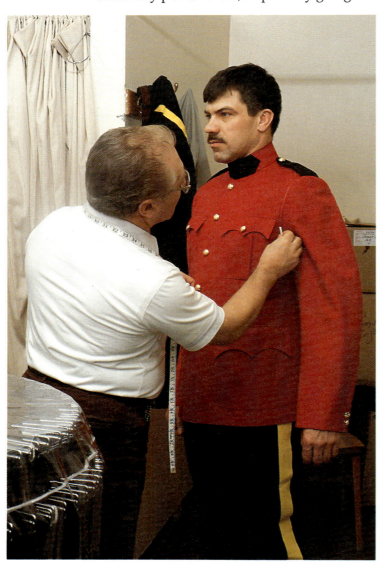

Pat Zunti being fitted for his red serge by the tailor. "If there had been another way to become a Mountie, I sure would have looked at it."

But then the Mounties called, and he was sworn in. He could hardly wait to get to his first detachment, but first he had to go to Montreal for six weeks of language training, and then he had to train for six months at the Academy. If there had been any other way to become a Mountie, he said, "I sure would have looked at it." But there was no other way, so he accepted his fate. When he came through the gate for the first time, he said to himself, "Welcome to hell."

Zunti and the rest of the recruits in Troop 17 knew they would be treated a lot better after they finished training. They came to the conclusion that there were two RCMPs, the rigid, traditional one preserved at the Academy, and the more reasonable and enlightened force they would be part of after they graduated.

The human rights revolution caught up with the Mounties in the 1970s and 1980s, but it still had a long way to go at the training academy in the 1990s. The major change in the regular force was that the people on the bottom were no longer almost completely under the thumb of those above them. They no longer complained with considerable justification, that the force "owned" them or that they had far fewer rights than criminals.

A federal commission of inquiry headed by Judge Rene Marin concluded in 1976 that the force was too strict in dealing with its personnel. It recommended the force shift its emphasis away from maintaining control over its members. The commission said that that may have been necessary when the force was young, but it was no longer appropriate or productive. Six years later, the Charter of Rights and Freedoms came into effect. This guaranteed the human rights of all citizens, and that included members of the force. A new RCMP Act was passed by Parliament in 1986 and came into effect in 1988. There were quite a few changes. New tribunals replaced the old "service courts," which were presided over by officers with vast powers and often dispensed arbitrary justice. Now trials had to be fair, and punishments commensurate with the offence. The practice of shipping members off to the middle of nowhere as punishment was curtailed. Mounties could file grievances, and their superiors were required to provide "guidance and correction" instead of punishment when they did something wrong.

These were revolutionary changes in an organization which had formerly been far more interested in maintaining its disciplined, rank-structured system than worrying about the rights of its members. Some of the changes had trickled down to the Academy, but tradition still held sway, and the time they spent in training was by far the most authoritarian experience the recruits were likely to encounter in the RCMP. It was almost as if they were caught in a time warp, leaving the rights-conscious civilian world, living like most Mounties did in the old days for the six months they were in training, and then suddenly being transported back to the modern era when they graduated.

"They're coming from a civilian way of life to a semi-military one, in actual fact probably more military than the military training that we see at Cornwallis on the east coast. It's a major change," said Staff Sergeant John Keyuk. He was one of the people who looked out for recruits' rights, such as they were, at the Academy. Keyuk was the "division representative." The RCMP doesn't have a labor union, as many other police forces do, but it has division reps like Keyuk who look out for the rights of the members. Technically, Keyuk was the recruits' advocate, since he was the rep for what had formerly been known as "Depot Division," which consisted of the training academy.

But Keyuk didn't interfere in the day-to-day process of training. He usually became involved with the recruits only if they got into big trouble — if they were going to be backtrooped or dismissed, for instance. For the most part, the recruits had nothing to do with him after he gave his lecture at orientation. They didn't even get to vote for him. He was elected by the instructors and others members of the force who worked at the Academy. Keyuk had been a self-defence instructor before taking on the division rep's job. He wasn't interested in using his position to be an ombudsman for the recruits or to make radical changes to the traditional training process.

"I could probably have a lot of what goes on here stopped," he said. "Take, for example, inspections of their dorms. Isn't it an invasion of their right to privacy to go in and inspect their residence without their permission, especially since they are required to pay rent for it?" But Keyuk felt that dorm inspections and the rest of the things that went on at the

Academy all helped to turn out good cops. "Staff members don't want to change it, and I don't want to change it, and if you ask the recruits, they'll tell you they don't want to change it, so why in the hell should we change it?"

But Keyuk didn't want to turn back the clock and give the recruits no rights at all. He recalled that when he was a recruit in the early 1970s, the Academy could hold a quick trial and convict a recruit of "disgraceful conduct," or he could be classified as "undesirable." Either way, he was quickly thrown out. Now they could not be thrown out without being given every chance to improve, and without all the proper procedures being followed. That's where Staff Sergeant Jim Turner came in.

Turner was the head of standards, the section with the "teeth." It was the only section with the power to recommend that a recruit be backtrooped or dismissed. It was standards which collected all the chits and the performance reports which were handed out by individual instructors. Standards was the clearing house for information on recruits, and standards called them in for a chat when there was any sign of trouble.

Most of the recruits said they didn't mind going to the sergeant major, because there was only so much he could do to you. You'd get your lecture and he'd confine you to barracks or make you write an essay, and that was the end of the matter. Standards was the place where you got called in for long, long talks with a performance evaluator, and it was standards which generated the paperwork which was the first stage in the process of backtrooping or dismissal. Turner was the one who spoke to the recruits in Troop 17 during orientation and told them they'd be offered a chance to resign before they were kicked out. It sounded harsh, but it gave a recruit an honorable way out, and a future employer would be told only that the recruit had served in the RCMP for a certain period of time and had left voluntarily.

Turner said that for a few years after the Charter of Rights came into effect, the pendulum swung too far in the opposite direction, and it was almost impossible to get rid of an unsuitable recruit. He was glad when it swung back to a more reasonable mid-point in the late 1980s. The problem was that after the Charter came into effect, the Academy had no mechanism to document that a recruit wasn't measuring up. The passing grade had been set at fifty for as long as anyone could remember, and that was so low that it was almost impossible for a recruit to fail academically. There was also no formal system of monitoring individual performance. Only one big file was kept on each troop, and no records were kept of how individuals performed in training, Turner explained.

There was plenty of informal evaluation going on, but it was not systematic and it was not documented. An instructor would notice something, and he would tell the recruit to smarten up and maybe mention it to the higher ups. Or he would punish the whole troop for the shortcomings of one member, and the troop would take care of the problem internally. If things didn't work out, the recruit was called in and given the boot, and that was the end of it. It was the same kind of arbitrary justice which had existed in the whole force. But that way of doing things would no longer do, not even in the Academy, which had been given so little thought in the new scheme of things that it was not even mentioned in the new RCMP Act.

The result was that for a few years in the late 1980s, failure and dismissal from the Academy were almost unheard of. Everybody who got in and managed to tough it out for six months graduated. But that changed when the passing grade was raised in most subjects to seventy or seventy-five, and when the standards office was established and started monitoring individuals. "Nobody slips through the system now," said Turner. "Each person is judged as an individual as opposed to the troop concept. Now we can spot those needing corrective training, and those who need to be removed from the troop or backtrooped." He said the mechanism was also in place to dismiss a recruit from the force. The standards section could document the recruit's inadequacies and the force's efforts to help the recruit overcome them.

But it rarely came to that. The usual procedure was to call the recruit in and level with him, as had been done in Len Peters' case and Cathy Crow's case. Faced with the prospect of going through the dismissal procedure, most recruits took the option of resigning, or agreed to being backtrooped or pulled out of training so they could receive special help.

The recruits in Troop 17 didn't spend much time worrying about violations of their rights, except once, when they were told they had to get rid of their sleeping bags. They slept in the bags on top of their beds so they wouldn't have to make their beds each morning. They stored the sleeping bags in their blue steel trunks, where they were permitted to keep their personal property. They were ordered to get rid of the sleeping bags, and kicked up a fuss about their rights being violated. They felt they had a right to use the sleeping bags if they wanted to, but the brass said the bags constituted a health hazard, and the force had the right to enforce standards of hygiene. The bags were dirty and smelly, because they were not washed or dry cleaned and sat in the unventilated trunks all day.

The recruits were told that the bags had to go, and that if they wanted to make a big deal about it, they might also have to give up their storage trunks, too. They knuckled under and got rid of the bags, and that was the end of the matter. This brief rebellion was an exception. For the most part, they went along with everything that they were told to do. They bitched a lot, but they accepted it all, throwing up their hands and saying they had no choice, or making the argument that the force had been in the Mountie-making business for a long time and knew what it was doing.

The recruits eventually came to accept almost everything about the Academy. One of the most startling transformations was their eventual compliance to dorm life. When they arrived, most of the recruits were used to having their own apartments, and several of the married ones had their own houses. They initially said they hated the cramped quarters and the lack of privacy in the long, narrow dormitory.

John Babbitt's sentiments were typical. "It stinks," he said after he had been living in the barracks for about six weeks. "There's no other way of putting it. There's no time to be alone, to escape it all. There's usually at least one, two, three other guys in there at the same time,

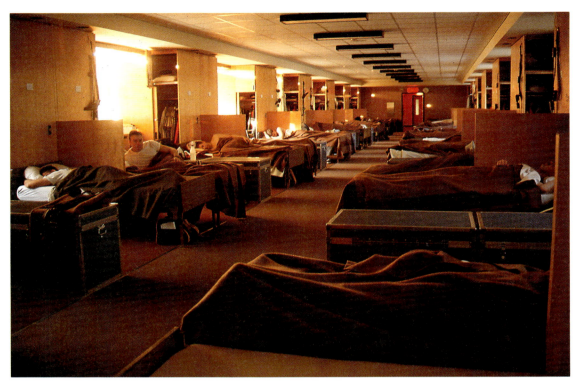
Early morning in the men's dorm. Communal living is one of the biggest adjustments recruits must face.

and they're all doing their own thing somewhere and I'm doing my thing elsewhere, and you can't really escape it. There's a huge washroom you've got to share with everybody. When I went home last week it was the first time in six weeks I showered by myself."

But the dorm was the centre of their lives. It was not only where they slept, but also where they made most of their group decisions and where they grew close to one another. They came to see the advantages of dorm life, and ultimately said they would prefer it to having their own rooms, an option which was being considered for the future at the Academy.

The dorm was a long, narrow room. It had a heavy steel door at one end and the communal bathroom at the other. The entrance had a sign outside requesting that women please knock before entering. The recruits were grouped in pairs, and each pair shared an area about eight and a half feet square. This was their space, and it was known as their "pit." They were "pit partners," and a strong bond usually developed between them. Their pit was bounded on the sides by their beds, and in the middle they kept the blue metal storage trunks where they had stashed their sleeping bags. They used their trunks to store some of their personal effects such as clothes, books and sports equipment, and many of them used the inside lids of their trunks to display pin-up pictures, artwork sent to them by their kids and calendars to mark off the days they had left in training.

At the back of the pit there was a combination bureau and desk called a chiffonier, in which they kept their socks, underwear, books and other things. The recruits had to arrange these items so that they formed a mirror image of their pit partner's layout. Many of them kept photos of their girlfriends, wives and children on top of their chiffoniers, providing a touch of individuality in the otherwise identical living spaces. They were also permitted to keep a radio and a clock on the shelf, but otherwise the chiffoniers had to remain clear. At the ends of each chiffonier were the wooden cupboards which the drill corporals took so much delight in checking. This was where the recruits kept their uniforms and civilian clothes.

Everything had to be arranged just so, with the shoes and boots lined up and laced up, the shirts all buttoned and facing the same way, and the hangers an equal distance apart. Shelves were designated for a boot-polishing kit, toilet articles and so forth, with the top shelf reserved for a wooden rack holding their Stetson hats.

There were sixteen pits in each dormitory, so a full troop of thirty-two could be accommodated, but since there were only twenty-eight men in Troop 17, and twenty-seven after Len Peters left, some of the places in their dorm were empty. But they couldn't take advantage of the extra space. The vacant spots had to remain unoccupied, and the recruits who slept near them had to keep them clean.

The beds of one pit were right next to the beds of the adjacent pit. The only thing separating them was a twenty-eight-inch-high board, so their heads weren't right next to one another when they slept. These were known as "snore boards," and they provided a minimum of privacy.

❖ ❖ ❖

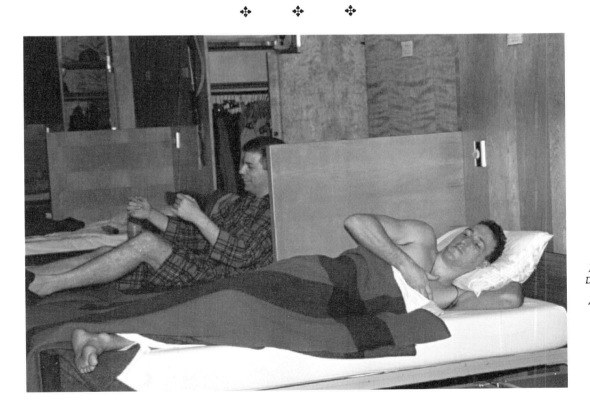

John Christensen and Don Davidson struggle out of bed. A small "snore board" between the beds offers what little privacy there is to dorm life.

~87~

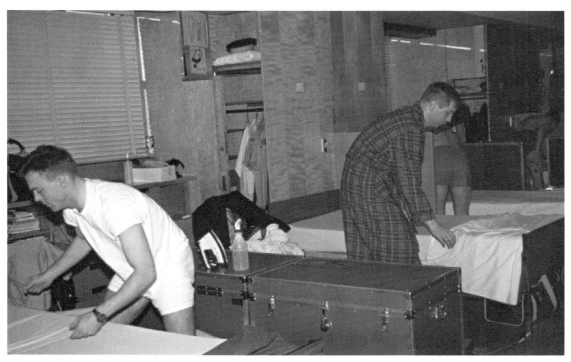

Pit partners Keith Blake and John Christensen make their beds. The pit is the area encompassing their beds, desks and storage trunks. Partners are jointly responsible for keeping their area clean.

Joe Kohut at work studying. Eventually, Kohut rented an apartment in downtown Regina.

Dave Attew and Dan Thorne give Marty Schneider some improptu help with his self-defence homework.

As their training progressed, the recruits came to think of the Academy as a big game. They realized that their instructors manipulated things to motivate them and keep the game interesting. Their clothing was part of the game. They started out wearing brown pants and running shoes because they were deemed "unworthy" to dress as real Mounties. The runners and baggy brown trousers identified them as beginners and made them feel like buffoons. They had to earn the right to wear the force's regulation high brown boots and blue trousers with the yellow stripe down the side. This was known as getting their blues. A troop normally got its blues about halfway through training, but the date was uncertain. A good troop could get its blues early, while a poor troop would have to keep trying until it was good enough, no matter how many weeks it had been there. There was always the possibility that a troop would be so bad that it would be labelled a "shit troop," and it wouldn't get its blues until long after more junior troops had theirs.

The recruits in Troop 17 thought they were a cut above average, and were hoping to get their blues early. It was a carrot dangled in front of them to encourage good performance. They wanted to win their blues before going home for the Christmas break, and anticipation ran high in the last drill class before the holiday. But Ferguson sent them on their way without a word about their blues, and they were disappointed. He gave them their blues a couple of weeks after they got back to the Academy in January. The recruits were ecstatic, convinced that they had finally earned his respect, which was very important to them. But the way Ferguson saw it, they were quite an ordinary troop and did not rate getting their blues before Christmas, when they had only been in training for about two and a half months. Besides, if he had given them their blues then, he would not have been able to use the incentive to motivate the troop after the holiday.

A month or so later, Ferguson "pulled" their blues when they did something wrong. It was a common tactic employed by drill instructors to keep a troop on its toes, the negative motivator in the old carrot and stick game. Troop 17 lost their blues when they came marching around the corner one day and unexpectedly ran into the commanding officer. They failed to salute properly, and soon got the word that Ferguson had decreed that they were to put their baggy brown pants and the running shoes back on. A few days later, they got their blues back.

❖   ❖   ❖

Trevor MacKay enjoyed playing the game. He got into trouble all the time for laughing in drill class, but it wasn't serious trouble, because it was okay to laugh if the corporal said something funny, which he often did. "There are a lot of funny things around here," said MacKay, a twenty-one-year-old with a brushcut and an impish grin. "There are sidewalks you're not allowed to walk on, doors you're not allowed to open. I laughed at myself the other day when I got all excited because I couldn't find my tie. It's really something the way people get stressed out around here and get upset over nothing. I try to deal with it by seeing the funny side."

MacKay got the last laugh when he was accepted by the RCMP. He had attended a community college in Ontario, and his instructors had told him he didn't have what it took to be a cop. "I had an interview with five teachers and they said I wasn't suited to be a police officer," he recalled. He was not permitted to study policing at the college. They stuck him in a program called "law and security administration."

"It kind of discouraged me a bit, but I knew deep down inside I wanted to do this," he said one Sunday afternoon after he had been at the Academy for about four months. "One

Despite being in dress uniform, errors in drill aren't tolerated. The recruits get a laugh at Mark Davidson's expense.

of my college instructors was a former member of the RCMP. He tried to prepare me to be turned down. Every time I'd move another step ahead in the selection process, he'd say that a lot of people get that far, but they don't make it into the force." Two weeks after he graduated from the community college, he was accepted by the RCMP.

He went to Montreal for language training, "but it didn't set in that I was a Mountie. I felt more like a student learning French." He still didn't feel like a Mountie as he drove from his home in Trenton, Ontario, to Regina, where he had arranged to meet another young recruit, Mark Davidson, at a gas station across the street from the entrance to the Academy. "Mark and I wanted to come in together," MacKay explained. He and Davidson had met on a bus in Montreal. They looked at each other and just knew they had more in common than their youth and their short hair. They quickly became pals, and their friendship had grown as they went through training together in Troop 17.

Davidson was nicknamed "Brown Nose" by his troopmates, partly to distinguish him from Don Davidson, who was dubbed "Big Nose" because of his prominent proboscis, but also because Mark was a keener. Some of his troopmates thought he toadied up to the instructors too much. He thought being a Mountie was the best thing in the world, and was already dreaming of returning to the Academy someday as a drill instructor.

Trevor MacKay enjoyed playing the game. "There are a lot of funny things around here. There are sidewalks you're not allowed to walk on, doors you're not allowed to open. I laughed at myself the other day when I got all excited because I couldn't find my tie."

Davidson idolized Ferguson, and rejoiced when he gave the troop permission to move up from brown pants and running shoes. "You go by a corporal in your blues and high browns and he says, 'Hi, guys.' That means a lot. He's acknowledging you, and you've won his respect." While many of the other younger members of the troop went out drinking at night and on the weekend, Davidson usually stayed in the barracks. "I'll be polishing my boots or cleaning my gun or doing homework, or I'll rent a movie and watch it," he said. He was planning to get married right after graduation, and didn't have a lot of money to waste going out. He had also lost interest in the wild life, and explained this by saying the Academy had changed him a lot.

"I didn't notice a change before leaving here at Christmas. If you'd asked me, I would have said I hadn't changed because everybody in the whole dorm changed together. But my parents noticed it. The values and things I used to find important to me just weren't anymore."

He and his friends used to go to a coffee shop around the corner from where he lived in St. Catharines, Ontario. "Everyone would meet there and spend an hour having a cup of coffee, planning what they were going to do, and off you'd go. A lot of times, if you said something that could be misread it was misread, and then it was a big joke. Or we would be yelling and screaming across the coffee shop like we owned the place. It was adolescent behavior."

When he went home for Christmas, he went back to the coffee shop. "Within twenty minutes, I said I'm outta here. I just couldn't do it. It wasn't because I felt like I was better than everybody, but when you live with twenty or thirty grown men, or who are growing up to be men in a short time, it's just not there anymore." Davidson said he had lost interest in his former friends, and they had little use for him. "I guess they couldn't stand the fact that they had stayed back and were still doing the same thing, and I had jumped forward. A lot of them were twenty-four or twenty-five years old, and they had dead-end jobs, but I was going someplace."

Davidson said his values had changed. He had a wedding to pay for and he was looking forward to supporting a family. "I can't afford to go drinking every night, and I'm not one to do that anyway. I like to stay home and get work done. I don't like to push stuff to the side. It just causes more problems." He concluded that he was growing up. "I've not only come here to become a cop, I've also come here to become a man."

chapter five

"I have to play by their rules, bite my tongue and go with the flow."

The dead man dangling from a rope has a bloody hole in his chest. His tongue protrudes and his trousers are down around his ankles. A shotgun lies about fifteen feet from the corpse. Was it murder or suicide? The recruits study the gory photo, and Corporal Henry Kinsella invites comments.

About three-quarters of them think it was murder, probably the work of a sex offender. The rest think the middle-aged man killed himself. They give reasons for their opinions and try to account for various pieces of evidence they noted in the picture. "You're beginning to do what police officers do in situations like this," Kinsella tells them. "There's a lot of discussion among the investigators. They consider all the possibilities, and don't dismiss anything without examining all the physical evidence."

Garret Hoogestraat and Pat Zunti discuss possible answers to Corporal Henry Kinsella's question.

Kinsella provides them with additional evidence. A second picture reveals powder burns on the victim's shirt, indicating he was shot at close range. A third shows metal fragments on his hands match the filings from the sawed-off shotgun barrel found nearby. Police concluded that the man cut the barrel so he could put the gun to his chest and pull the trigger with his thumb. He put the noose around his neck to be sure he would die if the shotgun didn't kill him.

Kinsella says good police investigators don't quit until they answer all the questions. How did the gun get so far from the body? Recoil flung it away. And the trousers dropped down around his ankles? "He had a bit of a belly like I do," explains Kinsella. "When his muscles relaxed, his pants fell down."

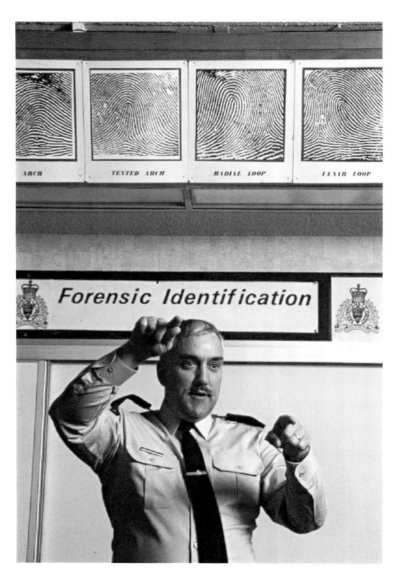

Corporal Kinsella explains the intricacies of identification. "If you dont have a sense of humor . . . it can be pretty tough on you psychologically." —Kinsella

All of Troop 17's instructors were like Kinsella, interesting teachers and specialists in their field. They stayed at the Academy for three or four years, and then returned to regular duties. New teachers with fresh ideas and current experience replace them. When a job opened up at the Academy, there were as many as 400 applications from across Canada. Many Mounties wanted to return to the place where they started their careers. It was a prestigious appointment and a good career move. A posting to the Academy usually meant a promotion from constable to corporal.

Kinsella was an identification expert, an "ident man" in the jargon of the profession. His job included showing the recruits how to take fingerprints and photographs and prepare diagrams of accident and crime scenes. He covered the latest DNA identification techniques, and told them how to deal with occupational hazards like chemicals and AIDS. He demonstrated how paint chips and clothing fibres could tie suspects to crimes, and told the recruits what they should do if they were the first police officers to arrive at the scene of a sudden death.

Garret Hoogestraat, John Babbitt and Pat Zunti. "Some of the areas we get into are kind of morbid." — Kinsella

A friendly man with greying hair, Kinsella tried to pass on his enthusiasm for his often gruesome work. He told the class about another suicide case. "We looked in the walls, the ceiling, the sheets, everywhere. There were only two places the bullet could be — in the man's head or in the big pool of blood beside it. I put on a rubber glove and ran my hand around in the blood," he recalled, wriggling his nose in disgust, "but I didn't find anything. They found the bullet in his brain later at the autopsy, but I had to be sure before we left the scene that it couldn't be anywhere else. You have to be thorough, even if it isn't always pleasant."

Kinsella conducted his classes informally. He didn't have anything against the spit-and-polish methods used elsewhere at the Academy, but preferred a more casual approach. In his first class with Troop 17, he asked them to introduce themselves, tell where they were from, and say when was the last time they had sexual relations. "Last time I was home," said one married recruit. "I'm still waiting for the first time," joked another. "What do you mean by sex?" asked a third. "None of your business," said a fourth. These were not the sort of things recruits usually said to their instructors, but Kinsella began this way to let the class know he wouldn't jump all over them for speaking out. Like all new recruits, the ones in Troop 17 soon became wary of being punished for doing something wrong. Kinsella wanted them to feel relaxed and spontaneous in his class, eager to learn rather than eager to please and anxious to avoid punishment. He knew that humor often helped to reduce tension. "Some of the areas we get into are kind of morbid," he said. "If you don't have a sense of humor, especially when you're in the field dealing with suicides and that sort of thing, it can be pretty tough on you psychologically."

Kinsella went through recruit training in 1973. He had minimal instruction in ident techniques, and during his early years in the force, he didn't feel comfortable at the scene of major crimes. "Those scenes used to scare the hell out of me," he recalled. He was afraid of touching the wrong thing or overlooking an important piece of evidence. But after eighteen years of experience as a Mountie, and specialized training in identification techniques, he had become confident, and tried to pass that attitude on to the recruits. "Whether it's a murder or something else, when you approach the scene, the wheels are already turning in your mind," he said. "You know essentially what could be there. Are you going to find tire tracks or fingerprints? Are you going to find blood, knife, hair? As long as you know what you're likely to find, it's much less of a problem."

Kinsella's approach was friendly and relaxed, but like the rest of the instructors, he followed the book. The teachers had a degree of latitude when it came to how they presented the material, but they had to follow a highly structured curriculum. Every class had specified "behavioral objectives" which were laid out by the RCMP training branch in Ottawa. These were explained by every instructor, usually at the beginning of each lesson. Generally the instructor projected a list of the objectives and the key points of the lesson on an overhead screen. These were the things the students would be tested on. The idea was that no matter who taught the class, the recruits would learn the same material. If an instructor was ill or got transferred halfway through a troop's training, it didn't matter. The next teacher could come in and pick up right where the other one left off.

It was a mechanistic approach, but it guaranteed conformity and helped the Academy pack a lot of information into a short period of time. Over the course of their training, recruits normally had to meet some 1,100 behavioral objectives, but this was reduced slightly in Troop 17's case, because eleven training days were cut from the normal twenty-six-week training program. Most of the troops which went through the Academy at that time had ten or eleven days cut from their programs because there was a shortage of Mounties in the field and the force wanted to get the recruits out to their detachments as quickly as possible. Most of the lost training time was cut from the swimming and physical education programs, and from a communications program called PIRS, the Police Information Retrieval System, which the recruits could learn later at their detachments.

The recruits were frequently tested to ensure that they met all the behavioral objectives. In practical subjects, these were usually tests of skill or endurance. In academic classes, the recruits had dozens of written exams. Some of the behavioral objectives were considered essential, and a perfect mark of 100 percent was required. That was the case when it came to basics like the circumstances under which a peace officer had the power to make an arrest. There was no room for error in such matters, so the recruits had to know this material cold. But most of their exams required them to score a minimum seventy-five. Many members of Troop 17 routinely racked up grades in the eighties or nineties.

Practical subjects like firearms had a minimum score. On the pistol range, for instance, the recruits had to get at least 200 out of a possible 300 points, but most were able to fire their .38-special revolvers a lot better than that. They usually shot at least 250, and many were up around 280.

There were examinations and "benchmarks" all the way through training. Those who failed were called onto the carpet, given remedial training and required to take the test again. They were warned that repeated poor performance would lead to backtrooping or dismissal.

The Academy ensured that the instructors, as well as the recruits, were up to snuff. Section heads monitored classes closely, sometimes telling the instructor they were coming to observe the class and sometimes dropping in unannounced. The instructors were evaluated according to the same sort of detailed criteria that were used to measure the performance of the recruits. The training officer, Superintendent Tony Antoniuk, kept a close watch on what was being taught and the people who were teaching it. He acted swiftly in the case of a married male instructor accused of having a sexual relationship with a female recruit in a troop that was ahead of Troop 17 in the training cycle. The instructor was pulled out of the classroom and assigned to administrative duties while the case moved through the force's disciplinary mechanism.

Antoniuk was a no-nonsense training officer who taught drill and shooting at the Academy in the 1960s, and then was rotated back to duties in the field. He won his commission and rose to command a sixty-four-member detachment in North Battleford, Saskatchewan, before coming back to the Academy as the training officer. He retired the same day that Troop 17 graduated.

Antoniuk said that years before his first stint at the Academy, instructors were not always outstanding in their areas of instruction. In the old days, he said, Mounties who were having trouble in their detachments were sometimes sent to Depot to get rid of them. That practice ended when the force adopted more business-like management practices and recognized that giving recruits the best-possible training was a good investment. Eventually, a year-long, two-part recruit training program was established. The first half was given at the Academy, and the second half took place in the detachments, where each recruit was teamed up with an experienced officer.

Training Officer Superintendent Tony Antoniuk keeps a close eye on what is being taught and the people who are teaching it.

Another improvement in training was the introduction of an instructional techniques course for Mounties who were appointed to the Academy's staff. In the old days, new teachers were just sent into the classrooms and expected to learn on the job. Most of them didn't have any idea how to present the material effectively. But by the time Troop 17 arrived, a two-week instructional techniques course was standard for teachers before they started working with recruits. The course taught them the basics, such as how to develop and follow a lesson plan, how to use audio-visual equipment, and how to create good rapport with students. Those who would be teaching drill, firearms, self-defence and driving also had to take what was known as a "potential." They had to go to the Academy for a try-out. Antoniuk and the instructors who were already teaching the subject decided if the candidate was good enough to join the staff. It was an effective way of weeding out people who looked good on paper, but didn't have the ability to get the material across effectively.

Betty Glassman called herself one of the "grammas" of the RCMP. She was in the first troop of female recruits who went through training after the force opened it ranks to women in 1974. After she graduated, she worked on highway patrol, town and city policing, plainclothes investigations and undercover surveillance before she was promoted to corporal and returned to the Academy as a driving instructor.

Glassman didn't start out wanting to be a police officer. "In my generation," she recalled, "women were secretaries, nurses or teachers. I chose to be a nurse, but once I got into nursing I began thinking about other fields. When the RCMP announced it was going to take women, I applied." She was one of thirty-two women from across Canada chosen to be in that first female troop. "I was twenty-six, and the third-oldest. There were two others who were thirty, then myself, and then they went all the way down to nineteen years of age."

The women were the centre of attention at the Academy and got so much media publicity, Glassman recalled, that "everyone seemed to hate us. There were 600 male recruits, and initially there wasn't a very good feeling of acceptance, although eventually they did accept us and actually became protective of us. All the instructors were men, and at first they didn't appear to like us at all or want us there either, but finally they, too, seemed to come to the conclusion that we were okay. We learned later that prior to their arrival, all the male recruits and instructors were herded into the drill hall and given a list of dos and don'ts. You will not swear. You will not call them names. Everything was going to change in that respect. You can imagine the hostility that went with that. But once they got to know us, they treated us all right."

When Glassman was a recruit, she was a lot like the people who followed her seventeen years later in Troop 17. She didn't like a lot of things that happened to her, but she went along with it because she wanted to be a Mountie. "I continually would say to myself, 'This is their game. I have to play by their rules, bite my tongue and go with the flow.' I had gone through nurses' training and lived in residence. I'd already had to live by the rules, and it wasn't difficult for me to make the transition at Depot."

She did well in most parts of her training, but had some unhappy memories of the drill hall. She wasn't her troop's right marker, but marched in the marker's position in drill class, and the instructor yelled at her a lot. "He wasn't abusive. It was just loud and boisterous and directed toward me. At first I would take it to heart, but then you grow a bit of a shell. That's part of the game. But one day, for some reason, I was having a particularly bad day, and he said something. I don't even remember what he said, but it was the last straw, and I broke down and cried. He was just flabbergasted. He didn't know what to do or what to say, so he just dismissed the class."

As an instructor, Glassman was treated a lot better than she had been when she was a recruit at the Academy. But even though she was on the staff, she believed in standing up for herself. She wore nail polish while she was in uniform, even though it was against the rules. She thought the prohibition against polish was an infringement on her rights, but she never made a big deal about it. "I wear light-colored nail polish which doesn't attract a lot of attention," she noted.

Corporal Betty Glassman gives instruction on the fine points of negotiating the Academy's serpentine road track.

Before coming to the Academy, she filed a grievance after she was passed over for a supervisory position which she had applied for in Alberta. The job went to a man with less experience, and Glassman was irritated when her superiors refused to tell her why she didn't get the posting. Using the force's grievance procedure, she went higher and higher up the ladder of command seeking an answer, and thought about exercising her right to take it all the way to the commissioner at the top of the RCMP hierarchy. But she backed off after being given a "friendly warning" by a senior officer that she could get labelled as a whiner if she persisted, and that could damage her career.

She felt there was a "double standard" in the RCMP. She believed that female Mounties were expected to be more virtuous than males. If men went out with women, they were generally admired by their fellow-Mounties and kidded about their sexual conquests. But women in the force couldn't even go out on dates without being subjected to a lot of snide remarks and talk behind their backs, she had discovered.

Paul Gilligan runs to set up a pylon knocked down on the driving course.

Glassman said there was also a double standard in that women were not given as many chances as men to prove themselves. She recalled when she was in plain clothes. The sergeant in charge of her section kept ignoring her when the time came to send out investigators on an important case, and kept putting her off when she asked to be given a chance. She finally got a shot at it only when there wasn't another person left in the office. She did well, and after that she became a regular member of the team, but she resented not having a chance to prove herself earlier.

She said that sometimes she thought her middle name was "Token," because she's been called a token female so many times. "It's been there right from the beginning, from the time when they decided to let us into Depot. We were all branded as the token women. Everywhere we went after that, it was the same thing. We were the first women to go into the detachments, the first to gain seniority, and now the first to come back to Depot as instructors. We do the same job as the men, but some people say we're here because the force is trying to look good and it needs to have token women at the Academy."

She recalled being offered a chance to go into plain-clothes work just a few years after she graduated. She turned it down and the job went to a man. "Here I was turning it down because I was thinking of how these guys with more seniority are going to feel, and maybe somebody deserved it more than me. Well, the guy who got it certainly never came to me and said, 'Thank you very much, Betty, for doing that.' I learned a lesson there, and after that I even got over the token thing. If you want to give me preferential treatment, bring it on, boys, because if I don't take it the next guy's going to, and he's not going to look back."

Mark Skotnicki out on a night drive in downtown Regina. Recruits are expected to log hours of driving practice on their own time. The unmarked blue patrol car is a familiar sight in Regina.

Glenn Miller, like Betty Glassman, had been called a token. He was the only native Indian at Depot when he was a recruit in 1972, and the only Indian on staff when he came back to teach in 1991. But talk about tokenism didn't bother him. He was easy-going, and took things as they came. Unlike most of the other instructors, Miller didn't have to win a competition to gain his position at the Academy. He was invited to apply, and while his race was never officially mentioned, he believed it was the main reason for the invitation. He knew he had a good record of service, but so did a lot of other people. "They wanted an Indian instructor," he said simply. "They want to get all ethnic groups in here working."

Miller was born in Ontario, but grew up on an Indian reserve just across the American border in Niagara Falls, New York. He joined the RCMP after serving four years with the United States Air Force. "One of the reasons I joined was to try and set an example for the younger kids," he said. "The conditions on a lot of reserves are very poor, and they don't have many good examples. I figure if I can influence the lives of one or two, I've done well."

He did undercover work and served in several detachments in the Maritimes and Western Canada during his nineteen years with the force. He was in charge of the RCMP office in the small western Saskatchewan community of Kyle when the invitation came to join the Academy's staff. "It's an honor to be here, but I was quite happy where I was," he said. "Most people usually want to be in charge of their own detachment. I finally got there, and then they wanted me to move here. It's hard on a family. We've moved three times in the last two years. I said to my wife, 'If you want to go, let's go, but if you don't, we'll stay here.'" His wife wanted to move, and Miller arrived just a couple of months before Troop 17 started training.

He was their human relations instructor. In some of his early classes, he plodded through the canned lessons, reciting the material that was set down in his book. It was often dull, and sometimes it seemed frustrating for both Miller and the recruits. But Miller gradually grew more confident and creative in his new role as an instructor, and after awhile his lessons got better. When he challenged the recruits to think, instead of just trying to pour information into their heads, the class came alive. A good example was his lesson on the Sikhs. The human relations curriculum contained sections on various ethnic groups, but the Sikhs were a particularly hot topic. The RCMP commissioner, Norman Inkster, had recently decided to permit Sikhs members of the force to wear turbans while they were in uniform. The first Sikh recruit to do so was Baltej Dhillon. He was in Troop 20, about five weeks behind Troop 17 in the training cycle.

The decision to let the Sikhs wear turbans was controversial, with many people claiming that it destroyed RCMP traditions, let minorities impose their will on the national police force, and introduced politics into policing. People on the other side of the debate said it showed the RCMP respected individual differences and religious beliefs, and was taking steps to encourage racial minorities to join the force.

Most members of Troop 17 were opposed to letting Sikhs wear turbans in uniform, and some of them had hostile attitudes toward Sikhs and other ethnic groups. Human relations classes were given at the Academy to provide recruits with information about various ethnic groups. The idea was not to try and force the recruits to change their attitudes, but rather to expose them to information so they could make informed decisions. It was a strategy Miller agreed with. He didn't feel he had suffered a lot of discrimination because he was an Indian. He had worked as a police officer both on Indian reserves and in mainly-white communities, and had generally found that he was seen as a Mountie first, and an Indian second. "But there have been a few times in a tense situation, like a bar fight, when people have said 'f-ing Indian' and that sort of thing. It doesn't bother me. I just consider it their ignorance."

Miller started the class in the prescribed manner. He presented a string of behavioral objectives, outlining what the recruits were required to learn for the exam. These included "list and explain the five Sikh religious symbols and their significance" and "explain briefly the Sikh common views or beliefs toward the Canadian criminal justice system, Canadian police agencies, and areas of conflict/perception." It was dry, factual stuff, but things soon livened up.

Miller told the recruits it wasn't the turban that was crucial to Sikhs. It was covering their hair that was important. Covering their hair was a sign that they accepted God, and Miller said a police officer should keep that in mind. If he arrested a Sikh, he should search the turban because it might conceal drugs, needles or razor blades, but Miller suggested the officer should be polite and ask the suspect to take his turban off, rather than ordering him to remove it or ripping it off his head. "You might also offer him a small cloth to put on his head," Miller suggested.

Glenn Miller taught human relation to Troop 17. His class covered everything from handling domestic disputes to dealing with different races and cultures.

This elicited plenty of discussion in the class. Some of the recruits demanded to know why Sikhs should be given that kind of "special treatment." They made a few racial remarks, and Miller warned them that openly expressing hostility toward Sikhs or other groups could get them into trouble. "You can think it," he told them, "but if you bring it out into the open, your career might suffer." He said it was smart police work, and not a sign of weakness, to be courteous and explain to a Sikh suspect what was being done, instead of just going ahead and searching the turban. Miller said police officers should show respect for all people they deal with, and avoid violence whenever possible. "It's a lot easier to talk than to fight."

The discussion expanded to how police officers should conduct themselves when they were in Sikh homes. Miller told the class that many Sikh houses have prayer rooms, and suggested that police officers should ask permission before entering the room. They might also remove their hats and take off their shoes, in accordance with Sikh custom. These ideas riled several of the recruits. "I'm in my own country," said one. "Why should I be extra nice to a Sikh person when I wouldn't be extra nice to a white male?" asked another. "You're there to do a job. You're not there regarding anything to do with religion," maintained a third recruit.

Miller didn't tell them they were wrong, or accuse them of being racist. He simply countered their arguments with a pertinent question. "Why not?" he kept asking when they said they couldn't do this or they wouldn't do that. When they said they wouldn't take off their hats before entering the prayer room, Miller asked them why not. They said it would tie up their hands, and they had been told they should keep their hands clear so they could draw their guns quickly in an emergency. Miller agreed that police officers should look out for their own safety, but he offered a simple solution. "Set your hat down," he suggested.

Miller said if there was a good reason not to do something, the police officer shouldn't do it, but he shouldn't be insensitive, he shouldn't push his weight around and abuse his authority, and he shouldn't be ruled by prejudice and unreasonable hostility. "If at all possible," Miller concluded, "why not humor people? Be a nice guy if you can."

One of the recruits in Troop 17 knew a lot about prejudice and unreasonable hostility. Kerry Mah had grown up with it. Mah's parents and grandparents came from China in the 1920s and paid the discriminatory $500 "head tax" the government imposed on Orientals at the time. They settled in Wainwright, Alberta, a small town near the Saskatchewan border where Mah was born.

"I was one of the few visible minorities in school." he recalled, "I used to get into fights three or four times a week. There was always someone with something to prove by beating me up. I learned a long time ago that if I was going to make it, I would have to prove myself."

Mah was five-foot-ten and weighed only 150 pounds, but he had learned how to fight well. It was useful experience in self-defence class. Many of the recruits had never been involved in a violent confrontation, and had difficulty when the instructors made them fight vigorously and inflict a good deal of pain on each other. Mah already knew about that. "When I was in elementary school, I had a lot of fights, but I didn't win too many. I wasn't a very big person. In junior high and high school, I had guys pull knives on me, but by then I had learned a few skills. I just turned it around and put it back to their throats." The physical attacks ended when Mah went to the University of Alberta to study engineering, "but when I would be walking with a girlfriend, you could see people turning around and making comments. They just couldn't accept a colored guy with a white girl."

After university, Mah worked for Petro Canada for about a year, and then went back to school to learn about computers. "I started my own computer consulting business and made really good money, but my parents got sick and they needed somebody to run the family restaurant. So I just picked up everything and went home." He joined the RCMP auxiliary in Wainwright. "They treated me like a regular member. They gave me special privileges to do a lot of things on my own. I'd work from maybe nine in the morning to ten or eleven at night in the restaurant, and then I'd go to the detachment and work to three or four in the morning, three or four nights a week."

Dave Rampersad points a shotgun at Kerry Mah in self-defence class. Growing up in rural Alberta prepared Mah for the physical confrontations in training. "There was always someone with something to prove by beating me up. I learned a long time ago if I was going to make it, I would have to prove myself."

Mah enjoyed police work. "It was the best experience for finding out what I was getting myself into by joining the force. I've gone out in the car and arrested people. I've been in bar fights. When I first started, I got a lot of racial remarks — gook, Chinaman, slant-eyes — I got a lot of that kind of stuff. At first I didn't know how I was supposed to react and I got frustrated, but as time went on I just learned to smile." That was one of the things the Academy stressed. Recruits had to learn to let insulting remarks roll off, whether they came from the drill instructor or anyone else. It was part of the self-discipline the trainees were expected to acquire. It didn't take Mah long to get the idea.

"You can say what you want and it doesn't bother me. Inside there's nothing. It doesn't affect me anymore. I'll never put myself in the position where I'll react to somebody calling me names, because it's not worth it. If I'm going to react to that, it just puts me on the same level that they're on."

Sometimes Mah and Dave Rampersad would joke about being the two "colored boys" in the troop. The others soon picked up on it, and there were a lot of remarks which sounded racist, but which Mah and Rampersad believed were meant in good fun.

Arron Polk and Kerry Mah ground fighting in self-defence class.

"I've told the people in our troop that if I can't take it from you," said Rampersad, "I can't take it from others. Say we're going to the shooting range, and Kerry and I happen to be in the back of the bus. We'll say, 'How come we ended up back here?' and somebody in the troop will yell, 'You colored guys are supposed to be in the back of the bus.' And we'll all get a laugh out of it."

Unlike Mah, Rampersad had experienced little racism when he was growing up. "When I came here from Trinidad, I was big for a thirteen-year-old, and that helped me. People didn't pick on me, and I had no problem with prejudice. You'd get one or two guys who would make the odd remark, but I went to school in Winnipeg; it wasn't a small town like where Kerry is from. It was a more multicultural area. The school was full of a lot of different ethnic groups, so it wasn't bad for me."

Rampersad made friends with people from all races. "We were all just a bunch of guys from school. White guys, black guys, brown guys, yellow guys. Everybody sort of respected each other. I was lucky when I was growing up, but I know there's a lot of prejudice and racism around. All you've got to do is read the paper." He thought he would likely experience some hostility soon after he graduated and went to his first detachment. "Being an RCMP and also being a visible minority is going to shock a few people," he predicted.

Rampersad wasn't bothered by racial remarks, but his physical condition was more of a problem. He was often called a "fat beach ball" and other names which made fun of his size. When he started training, the five-foot-ten Rampersad weighed 210 pounds. He had a pot belly, and found his physical classes especially hard. His instructors gave him a lot of compulsory training, and Rampersad got tagged with the nickname of "Mr. Mandatory." He had mandatory swimming, mandatory self-defence, mandatory firearms and mandatory drill. Being weak in so many areas undermined his self-confidence.

"I thought I had really poor abilities. I phoned my Mum and I started crying. I don't usually cry on the phone. I don't usually cry at all, but I started crying to my Mum, and I said to her, 'I feel really bad, because it seems like everything I do, I get all these mandatories. I feel like a really dumb person. Everyone else seems to be so good at everything. I know I'm not as bad as I look, but it's just taking me more time than it's taking other people, and I don't like that.'"

His mother told him she believed in him, and said she knew he was going to make it. "Go with the flow," she told him. "Try your best. I know you can do it." And she was right. By the time he had finished his sixth week of training, Rampersad had slimmed down to 187 pounds. He still had a lot of mandatories, but he was not letting them get him down. He saw them as opportunities to improve himself. He talked to his mother frequently, and gave her much of the credit for helping him get through the worst of it. "She'll write me letters, phone and send stuff. That really helps a lot. It keeps me going."

Rampersad also got a lot of support from others in his troop, and from Mah in particular. Dark skin wasn't the only thing they had in common. Mah also had a lot of mandatories. "There was one week when I didn't want to be here," Mah recalled. "I had mandatories in just about everything. But Dave and I just hit it off, and we helped each other through it.

They were two recruits near the bottom of the heap, and they helped each other. "It's lonely at the bottom, and it's nice to have somebody there with you. It's like you've had your hardest day ever, and everybody goes home and jumps in their bed back at the dorm, and we've got to get up, because we've got three mandatories a night. We come back to the dorm after classes end, change our clothes, go and have supper, and then we go swimming," said Rampersad. "Then we go to self-defence, because it's in the same building, and then we rush over to firearms. It's no color thing. It's just that we have the same mandatories, and we do them together."

❖   ❖   ❖

Kerry Mah helps Dave Rampersad adjust his tunic. "Dave and I just hit it off, and we helped each other get through." — Mah

The recruits were dog tired one afternoon. A lecture on drugs and the law could have put them to sleep, but Corporal Pat Kamenka caught their interest right away. He asked if they had seen the television commercial featuring Juan Valdez, the Columbian coffee grower. "Maybe Juan is smiling about more than coffee," he joked, winking and mugging like an owl behind his thin-framed glasses. The class howled. Then he became Detective Sonny Crockett on the television show *Miami Vice*, shoving his finger into an imaginary bag of cocaine, poking his finger into his mouth, smacking his lips, rolling his eyes, and proclaiming, "That's good shit, Tubbs!" More laughs. Then he told them about a young Mountie who searched a car and found a bag containing small pieces of paper. The inexperienced cop couldn't imagine why the guy would have a bag of confetti. "No wedding around, no bride, no groom," deadpanned Kamenka, scratching his head. He tossed the imaginary bits of paper onto the ground, and jumped back into the narrator's role, predicting that "there are going to be a lot of very happy cats and dogs around." The class roared.

That kind of opening was typical in Kamenka's class. The recruits felt he was one of their best teachers. They found him a welcome change from the stiff and stern routines that dominated their lives at the Academy. Kamenka got his points across with flair and good humor. He treated them with respect.

Law instructor Pat Kamenka. "If you mention something they are familiar with from television, or direct the humor toward some of the problems they have in training, it activates their minds."

~111~

Kamenka had an interesting background. He earned a degree in zoology and biochemistry from the University of Alberta, but when he graduated in 1970 there were few jobs for biologists. He ended up working for a company that trained bears for a subsidiary of the Walt Disney organization. "They would ship their grizzlies and cougars and jaguars up to the bush area. Our job was to train them so they'd attack people in movies. You'd have to teach the bear to bite on the shoulder and rip the jacket, but it looked like he was tearing at the ear. Then they wanted me to go down south and pretend to be a jungle boy in a movie. They wanted a big snake to drop out of the tree, put its coils around me and drag me into the swamp." Kamenka didn't like the sounds of that, so he quit and got a job chopping trees on the west coast until he joined the Mounties.

He had always wanted to be a policeman, but his father was against it. He hated cops. "Years ago, Dad was taking a neighbor to the hospital. She was pregnant. I don't know how much of an emergency it was, but Dad felt it was an emergency, and he drove through a stop sign. A policeman followed him to the hospital. Dad explained what he was doing, but the policeman gave him a ticket anyway, and after that, Dad had no time for police officers. For a long time he wasn't very happy that I joined the force, but eventually we made our peace."

Kamenka thought back to his own training days. "Some of the classes were very difficult if the instructor stayed specifically with the book or spoke in a monotone," he recalled. He remembered nodding off sometimes, especially in law class when the instructor just plodded through the material. Kamenka decided that he was going to teach law with some flair.

Don Davidson in law class. "The idea is to get them thinking as opposed to . . . 'I've got to sit still and straight or I'll get in trouble.'" — Kamenka

He kept up with the news, and used current events to illustrate points in his lectures. And he told a lot of jokes. He had a standing joke about a character he called Henry Lipshitz, Jr. Lipshitz was always getting into trouble over one thing or another, and Kamenka used him to illustrate his points.

"It can't turn into a stand-up comedy routine of yuk-yuks, but if you mention something they're familiar with from television, or direct the humor toward some of the problems they have in training, it activates their minds." When Kamenka was in training in 1974, some of his instructors insisted that the recruits sit at attention for the whole fifty-minute lesson. He preferred more activity, and let the recruits move around and stand at the back of the room if they felt sleepy. "The students are relaxed, but you can see whether they're interested or not if you look around. You have to be careful they don't become too relaxed. The idea is to get them thinking, 'What's he saying?' as opposed to, 'I've got to sit still and straight or I'm going to get into trouble.'"

The warm-up jokes in Kamenka's classes usually planted seeds for points he wanted to get across during his lesson. He returned to the people he mentioned at the beginning of the class and tied the lesson together. Juan Valdez, the Columbian coffee grower, was a good lead-in to a discussion on where all the drugs were coming from. The Sonny Crockett impersonation helped Kamenka illustrate what police officers should not do. He told them never to put powder which they suspected was drugs into their mouths. And he used the story about the little pieces of paper to give the recruits tips on how to recognize various forms of drugs. He explained that LSD was often put on bits of absorbent paper, and if you didn't know what to look for, you could mistake it for confetti. After Kamenka's class, the recruits weren't likely to make that mistake.

chapter six

"The fun and games are over, folks. It's all for real now."

One of the recruits didn't wait until he got to the training academy to prove he had the makings of a Mountie. The night before he left home for Regina, Lorin Lopetinsky, one of the youngest members of Troop 17, used a 12-gauge pump action shotgun to help an RCMP officer subdue three violent men.

Lopetinsky's family and friends in Lamonte, Alberta, had thrown a going-away party for him that Saturday afternoon. After it was over, he went for a drive and saw a police car rush by with its lights flashing. Lopetinsky was a member of the RCMP auxiliary, and thought the officer might need help. He picked up his nineteen-year-old brother and took off down Highway 15, the only road leading out of town. They soon came upon Constable Lorne Siba, who was in a tight spot. Three drunken men were advancing on Siba, who was holding a shotgun and warning them to back off or he would have to shoot.

"They were pretty crazy. One guy was known for the fact that he wanted to kill a cop," Lopetinsky said. "I jumped out of the truck and asked if I could help. Constable Siba handed me the shotgun and told me to hold the other two guys at bay." Lopetinsky had a cool head for a twenty-one-year-old, but he also had an intensity which suggested he meant business. When he ordered the two men to get down, they dropped to their stomachs and spread their arms out to the sides. Siba grabbed the third man and soon had him down on the ground too, but he struggled violently, Lopetinsky recalled. "I called my brother out of the truck. He helped put the guy in the cruiser."

Early the next morning, Lopetinsky left for Regina to start recruit training. He thought he would have to return to Lamonte to testify in court, but the two men he dealt with weren't charged, and the third man pleaded guilty and got six months in jail. Lopetinsky was given a written commendation praising him for being "instrumental in defusing a very violent situation which could easily have ended with tragic results."

The troop cheered when the citation was read out loud in class by one of the instructors. The members of the troop always made a big show of congratulating and supporting one another in public, but that didn't mean Lopetinsky was best buddies with them. "I can't really say I got really close with any of the guys here. I'm not close enough to anyone that if we were posted to the same place, I'd want to live with them. I can go out and have fun with them, but all my real friends are back home."

Like many others in the troop, Lopetinsky was lonely sometimes. He phoned home often and talked to his parents and brothers. He had a girlfriend back in Lamonte, but broke up with her while he was at the Academy. "She's in accounting and is going to be graduating this year. She's starting a new life, and I'm starting a new life. We're not ready to settle down. We're still friends," he said. He went out on a few dates with girls in Regina, and spent some nights at the Original California Club, but he didn't get seriously involved with anyone.

"The first couple of weeks you're here, you're popular as hell. The girls are all over you. They want to dance with you and get to know you. Now when you walk into the OCC, they just kind of look at you. They know who you are. You're just about to leave, so you're not very interesting."

Lopetinsky got away from the dormitory whenever he could. He would go home for the weekend, or rent a motel room in Regina. Often he just went out for a few hours in the evening. He'd drive around listening to music and relaxing. Some of the people in the dorm bothered him. He tried to get along with everybody, but he was an all-Mountie, gung-ho recruit. He didn't have much use for people who weren't as keen on the force as he was. "This may sound silly," he said, "but I take a lot of pride in the way I look in my uniform. You get the odd guy in here who won't polish his boots. He will say there's no use in doing it. That just bugs me. I'm proud of being here, and I don't like it when someone's not proud to be here and doesn't put forth the effort."

Lorin Lopetinsky always wanted to join the RCMP. "I can still remember in grade one . . . everytime I saw a police car go by I'd stand at the side of the road in awe."

~116~

He didn't want the system changed so that each recruit would be given a private room. "I think the dorm life is sheer hell, but what better way to mould people to work together as a unit? In the field you'll have to work with people you don't like. In my old job, I thought if I had to work with some of those guys for the rest of my life, I'd have killed them. They'd drive me nuts. But now, after living here with twenty-seven other guys, putting up with all their little quirks and them putting up with my little quirks, I could work with anyone. It's an excellent way of moulding people to be as one."

Lopetinsky said Troop 17 was made up of all kinds of personalties, and described his troopmates as "very much a collection of individualists. Quite a few of them are older, married guys. Imagine having to come here and live in a big room with twenty-seven other guys. You have to wear the same clothes and follow someone else's instructions. A lot of the guys had been living on their own for many years. It's hard for them. It's like going back home again and listening to your parents all over again."

In the beginning there was a lot of dissension, but over the months, he said, the group gradually came together. "I think our motley crew has finally turned into one liquid, flowing unit." He felt that as the end of training neared, Troop 17 had acquired a good reputation and was well regarded by the instructors. In Lopetinsky's mind, pleasing the instructors and

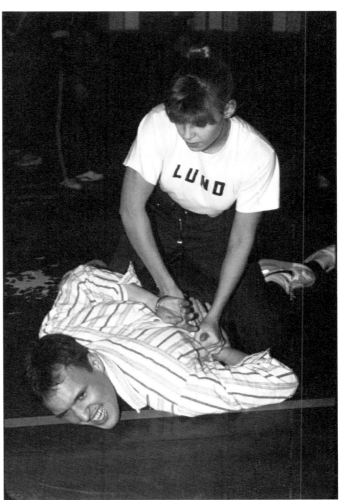

Suzanne Lund handcuffs Loren Lopetinsky.

winning their respect was vital. "I look at some of these other troops that have been trashed every second weekend since they got here. They have bad attitudes," he said. He felt Troop 17 had more self-discipline, and compared his troop to another one which was always getting into trouble. "They had their blues for three days and then they lost them. They just weren't listening."

He said Troop 17 had a lot of late-night meetings in the dorm as it struggled to get its act together. The meetings were spirited, but they were organized. The recruits had to raise their hands to speak. "Many nights we sat down and started screaming at each other. We had a good bitch session. We argued about a lot of stuff. It was basically conflicts of interest, like, 'Why should I have to listen to you? Why should I have to clean up someone else's mess?' Sometimes we talked it out and came up with a compromise, and sometimes it just didn't get resolved."

Lopetinsky would have put up with almost anything to become a Mountie. He had wanted to join the RCMP since he was a kid. "I can still remember in grade one, even before that, every time I saw a police car go by, I'd stand at the side of the road in awe." His father was a mechanic and his mother was a nurse. They were friends with a lot of Mounties, "and whenever they'd come over for coffee I'd sit there and look at the uniforms and get stars in my eyes." After he finished high school, he got a job in a rolling mill and joined the RCMP auxiliary. He went to accidents, domestic disputes and bar fights, and the regular members of the force soon took a liking to him and showed him how to handle weapons.

Within days of joining the auxiliary, he applied to become a regular member of the force, "but I really had no chance to get in when they were favoring university graduates and bilingual people. I was ecstatic when the force adopted a new policy, opening it up to give everybody an equal chance to be considered." Like the others, he went through a long selection procedure, and he was accepted just in time to meet a deadline he had set for himself. He had always hoped to become a police officer by the time he was twenty-two, and was scheduled to graduate three days before his twenty-second birthday.

But there was a hitch. One of the things the recruits had to do to make it through the Academy was pass the Cooper's test, which measured cardiovascular fitness. That meant running a mile and a half in ten minutes and forty-five seconds. Lopetinsky was young and strong, but early in training he seriously injured his right knee in self-defence class. "I was in a lot of pain, and couldn't run for about six weeks. Then slowly I got back into it."

He did poorly when he ran his first Cooper's test. "I did it in 12:13. I needed to do it in 10:45, so I had a long way to go. I ran my second Cooper's in 12:26, which was even more disastrous." The troop's physical education instructor, Corporal Gilles Levesque, put the pressure on Lopetinsky. He told him he would be faster if he used a wheelchair, and gave him a negative performance chit for each of his failures. Lopetinsky didn't think that was fair. "He knew I hurt my knee, but he was on my back. I really resented him for that. He kept on bugging me. I was really starting to feel bitter toward the man."

As the end of training approached, it came down to do or die for Lopetinsky. If he didn't pass the Cooper's test, he would be backtrooped, and he feared that would mean the end of his career in the Mounties. "I felt that if I didn't do it with the troop I was in, I wasn't going to do it at all." He went home for the weekend and talked to his parents and brothers, who were good athletes. "They told me how to control my breathing and how to deal with the pain. They told me to run with a corporal, and whatever I did, not to let that corporal beat me across the line." On the day he made his third and final try at the Cooper's test, he told Levesque that he was going to succeed. "I really psyched myself up. I was full of adrenalin, full of piss and vinegar. I told Corporal Levesque I was going to show him I could do it."

Lopetinsky and the rest of the troop began to run, along with one of the other physical education instructors, Corporal Terry Tycholis. "Usually I was toward the back of the troop, but this time I took off like a bat out of hell. I was passing people who usually passed me. It was the hardest I had ever run." The course looped around behind the Academy's shooting range, and that's where the one-mile mark was.

"If you get to that point in seven minutes, you'll make it if you can keep your pace up. Halfway around the loop, my knee started to give out and I was starting to lose my wind. All I could hear was Corporal Tycholis saying, 'Show me how much you want it.' He kept this up for me and Dan Thorne, who also had a bad knee and was running with me. He kept turning around and saying, 'Come on Thorne! Come on Lopetinsky! I want to see you guys do this.' My knee was swollen, but I kept pushing it. I kept thinking, 'I have to do it. I have to do it. If I don't do it now, I'm not going to do it ever.' I felt like the little engine that could."

And he did it. His time was 10:33. He had shaved a minute and forty seconds off his previous best time, and he had passed the Cooper's test with twelve seconds to spare. He said later that when people talked about the Academy being a place which brought out the best in recruits, they were talking about him. He had accomplished what he had once thought was impossible, and it made him feel like he could conquer the world.

His remarkable success on the Cooper's test led to a dramatic change in Lopetinsky's opinion of his physical education instructor. His bitterness toward Levesque was transformed into respect. Lopetinsky concluded that Levesque had been right to put pressure on him. "He was trying to motivate me. Now I think he's a fantastic man, one of the best instructors here."

Lopetinsky wasn't alone in his admiration of Levesque, a warm and energetic man who took obvious joy in his work. He joked that he was forty-three years old, but he had the heart of a nineteen-year-old. He was in superb physical condition.

He exuded vigor and self-confidence, and commanded the troop's respect. He demanded a lot from them, but was able to inspire the recruits and make them feel good about themselves. They put out extra effort for him, but he told them they should do it for themselves. "If you are willing to put a lot in," he said, "you will get a lot out. Don't do it for me or anybody else. Do it for yourself, only for you."

When Levesque assigned them to perform a demanding exercise, he urged them to do it joyfully, "because it's good for you." The troop soon picked up on the phrase, and sometimes when they were running, lifting weights or doing other exercises, one of the recruits would imitate Levesque's French accent and call out, "because it's good for you!"

Levesque's superiors sometimes accused him of being soft on trainees, but he felt the good results his troops were able to achieve proved the value of his methods. "I tell them at the beginning that they are like my family. In the first hour I say to them, 'Welcome to my class. We're strangers, but in the end, with good esprit de corps, and if you're a good troop that stays together, we will form a big family.'"

Levesque's attitude toward recruits was shaped by his upbringing. He grew up on a farm in Riviere-du-Loup, 120 miles east of Quebec City, and often worked with his father. "My dad didn't order me around or yell at me," Levesque recalled. "He asked me, 'Would you do that? Could you help me with this?' It was a good approach for me, and I find it's a good approach to use with the recruits. Sometimes I have to be really strict, but never stupid." Levesque felt it was stupid to be critical of recruits all the time, because it made them feel negative about themselves and depressed them. He recalled that some of his own physical

Mel Klatt, Pat Zunti, Bob Fremlin, Dave Dubnyk and Jason Kerr (l-r) on a timed run.

education instructors were always critical when he was going through the Academy as a recruit in 1973. He was in top shape and had no problems, "but I saw a lot of other people who were weak. They were doing their best, but instead of offering encouragement, the corporals always tried to run them down."

Levesque said Troop 17 had improved a lot since they started at the Academy. He noticed a big difference after Cathy Crow was pulled out of training. "A weak one pulls them all down. At the beginning, when they were warming up, Crow held the troop back for five minutes or so. It was the same when they were doing exercises. They were so hard

Physical education instructor Corporal Gilles Levesque. "Don't do it for me or anybody else; do it for yourself."

Ron Roberts found physical training tough. Exercise joyfully "because it's good for you!" — Levesque

~121~

for her, and she held everybody back." He blamed the RCMP's recruiting officers for letting people like Crow into the Academy. "Sometimes they miss the boat. To send us a person like that, an unfit person, not able to start the training, causes real problems."

Levesque felt that recruiters who approved the applications of unfit people weren't doing their jobs properly. "Maybe they're thinking that if you're not in shape, you'll get in shape when you get here. But this isn't the place to get in shape. You have to be in shape when you get here." He thought the problem would end when the force adopted a new physical testing procedure, which was supposed to be coming into effect soon.

A system called PARE, which was short for Physical Ability Requirement Evaluation, was being set up to replace the pushups, situps and stair-climbing exercises which were used to measure the fitness of Crow and the others who wound up in Troop 17. The PARE test was more directly related to police work. The new test included simulations of a chase, a struggle and an arrest, and unlike the old test, it did not have lower requirements for women than for men.

Paul Gilligan wasn't in good shape at the beginning of training. He was unco-ordinated and had less strength and stamina than most of the others in the troop. At twenty-nine, he was older than most of the others, and to make matters worse, he had broken his ankle the previous spring. That had prevented him from running, and running was the exercise he liked best. He had planned to do a lot of running to get in shape before he arrived at the Academy, but ended up sitting around for about two months waiting for his ankle to heal.

His physical weakness showed up quickly, and for the first month or so, it looked like Gilligan might not make it. His instructors put him on mandatory training in physical education, self-defence and drill. Gilligan had an expressive face, and he looked like he was in agony when he struggled to climb a rope in the gym or was wrestling with an opponent in self-defence class.

Sometimes he also appeared to be angry, giving the impression that he was stretched to the limit and that if he was pushed a little further, he might boil over. That was the sort of thing his instructors were watching for. One of the purposes of training was to weed out people who were physically or emotionally unsuited to be police officers. The idea was that it was better for them to crack in training than after they had graduated and were working in the field.

But Gilligan fooled a lot of people who thought he wasn't going to make it. He had a great deal of inner strength and determination, and he rose to the occasion.

Instead of letting his weakness get him down, he started building himself up. On a typical day, he would go through the regular classes, and after that, while many others in the troop were relaxing or studying, he would put in half an hour practising self-defence, and spend an hour doing exercises and lifting weights in the gym. He would then go back to the dorm, do 100 pushups and 100 situps, and go out for a run before going to bed.

It was exhausting, but it paid off. His strength gradually increased, and along with it he felt his self-confidence growing. One of the places where he proved himself was on the "challenge circuit" in the gym. It was a course set up to test the recruits' strength and endurance. It was a mixture of lifting weights and mat exercises. They did as much as they could in twelve minutes. The recruits called it "twelve minutes from hell."

The circuit started with double-elbow jackknife knee touches, and then there were military presses, double-thrust squats and stands, bar curls, leg exchange toe touches, and finally upright rowing exercises before the circuit started over again. They had to do twelve repetitions of each exercise before they could move on to the next exercise. If they got stuck on one of the weight-lifting exercises, they had to stop and rest and then continue until they did all twelve lifts before going on to the next station.

They got one point for each exercise they completed. The pass mark was 350. The top mark in Troop 17 was 440. Gilligan got 380. He was proud of himself for doing so well, and happy to discover that he wasn't at the bottom of the class in the challenge circuit or any of

"You're not the same person you were when you went in . . . You know your limitations." — Gilligan in self-defence class.

the other physical tests that they had to take. "It was nice to come up with a respectable score after doing all that work," Gilligan said.

He felt he had grown stronger mentally as well as physically. "You're not the same person you were when you went in. You're more confident. You know your limitations. They test you in everything every day here. They keep pushing, pushing, pushing." It was hard while he was going through it, Gilligan concluded, but in the end it gave him a lot of self-respect and a bond with other members of the force. "Going through Depot gives you a common origin. You're part of one big family. Everybody in the force has been through this. You can meet a Mountie anywhere and that's what you'll talk about. In a way, the worse it is at Depot, the better it is, because you can go through the rest of your life being proud of what you were able to put up with. You can't bullshit your way through here like you can at university. You either have the ability to do it or you don't."

Hard as he found the physical side of training, Gilligan said being away from his family was even worse. He and his wife Joan had a seven-year-old boy, Justin, and a four-year-old daughter, Jessica. They lived in Winnipeg. Gilligan said if he had been able to go home every night, "I wouldn't care what they did to me during the day. It's hard enough here, but when you add loneliness on top of it, and a feeling of guilt, it's really bad. Justin has had a rough time. I feel I should be taking him to play hockey. He's pretty lonely and frustrated. He really resents me for this. He's not the kind of kid you can explain things to and he says, 'Okay, Daddy, everything's okay.' He gets mad. He's damn pissed off about me being away."

Jessica and Joan were also having trouble adjusting. "When I first left, it was a lot of tears and, 'I miss you, Daddy.' Now when I go home it's a tug of war. My wife wants my attention and my kids want my attention, and even though my wife's thirty years old, she's not giving an inch of ground to the kids."

Gilligan felt especially badly about being away from his kids because his own father had little time for him when he was a boy. His father had worked in the RCMP security service. "I was the youngest of four children. When I was growing up, my old man didn't have a lot to do with me. He was going to university. He worked odd hours in the Mounties. He was always gone. Now my son's growing up, and it's the same with me as the father. I can understand how my son feels."

Gilligan left home the same day he finished high school. "I hated Toronto and was looking for an adventure. I went to Winnipeg and got a job working for Via Rail. I started washing dishes and ended up as a chef and the in-charge porter. We ran all over the country. I got married and had a child at age twenty-two, so the job wasn't so good because I was away from home a lot." After he left Via, he got a job as a groundskeeper and went to university at night. He got a degree in economics, then took certified management accounting classes, but he decided that wasn't what he wanted. "The idea of going to work in the commercial field, profits and banking and stuff like that, didn't interest me. I'm not motivated by whether some rich person with stock is making a profit."

He kept working as a groundskeeper, but he was often laid off and could see he wasn't getting anywhere. He started looking around for a job that would be interesting and give him a secure income. Until that point he had not thought about a police career, but one day he phoned the RCMP, and they told him to come down to the office and talk. Two years later, he was in training.

❖ ❖ ❖

One of the roughest classes for Gilligan and the rest of the troop was self-defence. The recruits called it "self-destruct," because it was where they were most likely to get injured. There was a constant flow of recruits from the self-defence gym to the Academy's medical treatment centre. Cracked ribs, twisted knees and dislocated fingers were so common that it was unusual to see Troop 17 without at least one of them wearing a sling or hobbling around on crutches. Corporal Barry Shannon was the instructor. He was nicknamed "The Bear," and with good reason. He stood six-foot-one and weighed 200 pounds, and he had a black belt in Tai Kwon Do. Shannon believed that a police officer should be aggressive. "My philosophy is that if you're productive out on the street, you're looking for people who are out there creating problems for other people, and so you are going to have altercations."

Shannon told the recruits to get ready for lots of fights once they started working as police officers. He had found that Canadians were generally becoming more violent and more

Injuries are common. Throughout training there was usually at least one recruit struggling with an injury.

likely to fight with the police. Some were just punks, but many were normally law-abiding citizens who had been watching too much television and had come to the conclusion that the thing to do was fight with the cops. This was especially true if they had been drinking too much. Shannon called it "liquor courage."

Shannon served in British Columbia and the Arctic before going to the Academy as an instructor. He had been in hundreds of fights. At jamboree time in Inuvik, he got into so many fights during a single shift that he sometimes lost count. "At the end of the night, I had the sleeves torn right off my patrol jacket and shirt." Even in quiet British Columbia communities, he found people who wanted to try their luck with the new cop in town. "It's almost like Andy of Mayberry when you drive into the town, but there are conflicts at every detachment."

As Shannon put it, "I've controlled all my fights," which was a diplomatic way of saying he had never lost one. He learned early in his career that there were two kinds of fighting — the kind that took place in gymnasiums and at martial arts tournaments, and the kind that police officers had in the streets and the bars. "Dancing around trying to grab a guy in a wrist lock isn't practical. It usually comes down to getting hold of some clothing, subduing the person and inflicting enough pain to make it unbearable for him to fight any longer."

Knee injuries abounded in Troop 17.

Self-defence instructor Corporal Barry Shannon demonstrates handcuffing techniques.

That's what the recruits did when they practised "ground fighting." It included everything except punching and kicking. They grabbed the hair and jerked their opponent's head back. They dug their fingers into the other person's eyes and pressed hard. Shannon made the little guys take on big guys, and the women fight the men. He taught them to grab their opponent's genitals and squeeze them hard to inflict a lot of pain.

Shannon worked them into it gradually, teaching them the basic techniques of attack and defence, and then having them practise on co-operative opponents until they got the hang of it. Then he made them fight with each other more and more vigorously, and soon he had them "go 100 percent," which meant fighting with all their strength. They kept at it until one signaled defeat by tapping his opponent on the shoulder.

Shannon told them to forget quaint notions about fighting fairly. A police officer couldn't afford to get involved in a long wrestling match. He would soon tire and wouldn't have enough energy to handcuff the bad guy and get him into the cruiser. The idea was to make the fight short and as unsweet as possible for the opponent. Pain was the key. Most people are not used to pain, Shannon said, and will do almost anything to relieve it. A police officer who knows how to inflict a great deal of pain will usually have short, successful fights.

They also learned why it was essential for them to fight to win their fights. "This isn't like back in school where the first person hit gets a bloody nose and the fight is over," Shannon pointed out. "You may have just stopped a person from committing an armed robbery. You've taken away his knife and you go to put the handcuffs on and the fight is on. There's nobody else around. He has access to your baton and your gun. Do you think if this person wins, he's going to let you hop back in your car and drive away?"

Shannon also taught them how to put pressure on the carotid arteries, which run up each side of the neck carrying blood to the brain. Pressing on the carotids can knock a person out in anywhere from two to fifteen seconds. He usually wakes up within a few seconds, but by that time he has been handcuffed. It's a good technique to use on people who are too drunk or high on drugs to feel much pain.

Shannon had used carotid control techniques more than 100 times in subduing suspects over the years, but one occasion stood out in his memory. Shannon was off duty and was waiting at a red light when a speeding car went out of control and rolled over. "I jumped out and was trying to be a good Samaritan. I went to see if anybody was still alive, and all of a sudden two guys were running away from the car. I looked at the licence and it was listed as a stolen car, so I yelled at them to stop. One of them all of a sudden had a gun in his hand. He turned around with his gun and I backed away."

The men ran off and Shannon followed them. "I knew that people would be phoning for the accident, and I was worried that one of our members was going to show up and get shot. I didn't realize that prior to this, there had been a shootout with Vancouver city police and high-speed chases all through Vancouver." The men had escaped from prison in the United States, where they were doing time for murder. "They went down an alley and jumped a couple of fences. I tried to keep up with them and keep them in view. At one point they tried to get into a garage, and I kept following as they went down the street trying to get into some cars."

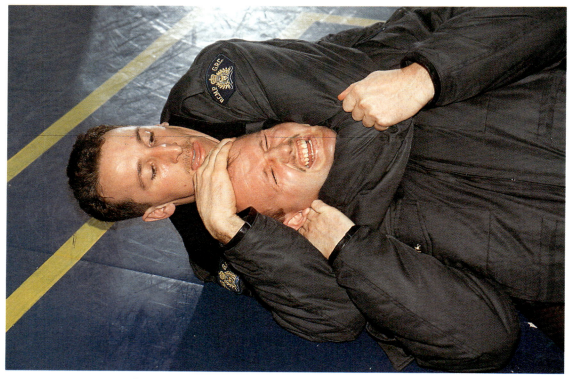

Don Davidson and Ron Roberts ground fighting. "Go 100 percent . . . and inflict enough pain to make it unbearable for him to fight any longer." — Shannon

Shannon was in full pursuit when the men suddenly turned around and started running back. "They confronted me. One had a gun and the other didn't. There was a lot of talking and yelling between them and me. Then the one with the gun started to pull out a second gun, like he was going to toss it to the other guy. I just had a gut feeling that if the guy who didn't have a gun got one, he would use it on me and I wouldn't be around much longer."

They were in the middle of an intersection, and Shannon had no place to run and hide. He grabbed the man who didn't have the gun and put pressure on his carotid arteries. "I took this guy out with everything I had. It took the gas out of him in a couple of seconds, kept him in front of me as a shield, and dragged him behind a truck." The man with the gun ran off, but other police officers soon caught him.

Some people said later that the unarmed Shannon was foolish to pursue the men, but he felt it was his duty. "You're not thinking about your own safety, I guess. You're so pumped with the idea that you're a trained police officer and that you have to protect the public, that you almost go a bit overboard sometimes."

❖ ❖ ❖

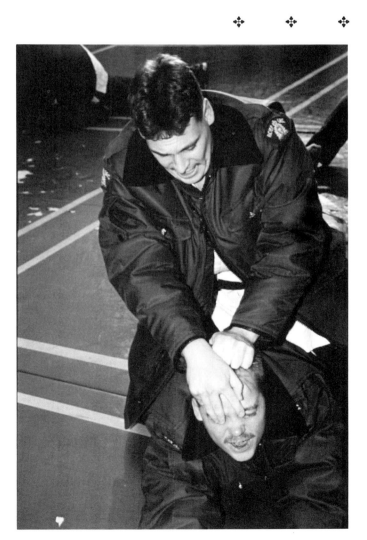

Mark Skotnicki and Arron Polk ground fighting.

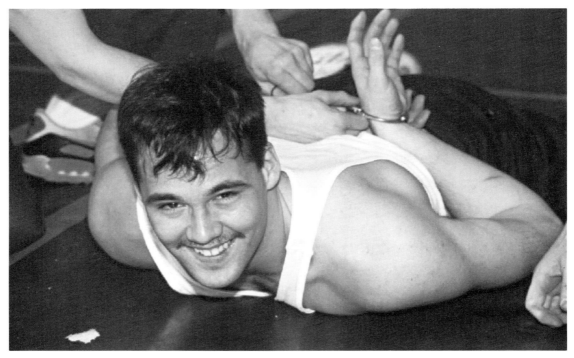

John Babbitt smiles after being handcuffed. Despite admonishment to fight 100 percent in self-defence class, one part of the recruits' mind knows it isn't serious. If it gets too tough you can always tap your opponent's shoulder to indicate surrender. Corporal Shannon pointed out that experienced street fighters know this too and might use it to get the upper hand in a confrontation. A quick tap on the shoulder, the police officer relaxes his grip, and the fight is on again.

Corporal Judy Best warned the recruits not to take chances and try to be heroes. She urged them to err on the side of caution, and told them that calling for back-up wasn't a sign that they were cowardly. Rather, it showed that they had good common sense.

Best was their "operational training" instructor. That meant she had primary responsibility for making sure that they left the Academy with an understanding of how to perform basic police work. That included such things as how to make arrests, read people their rights, search them, put them into cells and give evidence in court.

One of Best's jobs was to talk to the recruits about officer survival. She told them that police officers who get killed are often largely responsible for their own deaths. The public thinks of them as brave cops who died in the line of duty, but investigations have shown that dead officers have often made mistakes such as acting too quickly or failing to follow proper procedures.

Best showed them videos which were something like the shows that many of the recruits had seen on television. They were dramatizations of police officers in action, but with an essential difference. Shows like "Top Cops" almost always ended with the good guys winning, but in the dramatizations which Best showed, the outcomes weren't as happy. They showed police officers being gunned down and the bad guys escaping. After watching a few of these videos, the recruits came to see how quickly and easily police officers could be killed if they were careless.

Corporal Judy Best, operations training instructor, dealt with the day-to-day police procedures.

Constable Arron Polk and Brian Davison break up a pub brawl at the Stand Easy Lounge. Much of the second half of "ops training" had Troop 17 practising their skills on each other by participating in scenarios.

In one re-enactment, two complacent cops put a suspect in the back seat of their cruiser without searching or handcuffing him, and then called on the radio to find out if he was wanted for anything. As the dispatcher started to reply that he was wanted for murder, the man pulled out a gun and shot them. Another video featured police officers who had survived being cut with knives. One cop said he had taken his eyes off a suspect's hands for just a second, and before he knew it, the man "had filleted my entire face and neck."

Best showed the recruits that there were all kinds of ways that a cop could blow it. One guy was snoozing in the back of the cruiser while his partner drove around on patrol. He was still snoring when his partner went out on a call, but he was soon awakened by gunshots. He found his partner lying in a pool of blood. He got on the car radio and called for help, but he looked around helplessly when the dispatcher asked for his location. Because he had been asleep, he didn't know where he was. Another officer arrested a suspect at a break-in, cuffed him and put him in the back of the car. Then he relaxed instead of checking to see if there were others involved. A second man came out of the building and shot him.

The case that Best spent the most time on was the one which had led to the introduction of classes on officer survival at the Academy. Best had a special interest in this one because it involved Candy Smith, who had been a member of Best's troop when she went through training in 1977. Just six weeks after graduation, Smith was seriously wounded and another Mountie was killed in a shootout in Virden, Manitoba.

It was a slow winter night, and the officers were making routine checks of vehicle licence plates at the Countryside Motel. A white van had been reported stolen in Calgary the previous day. Two other officers approached Room twenty and knocked on the door while Smith and her partner stood nearby. The door opened and a man cut loose with a shotgun, killing one of the Mounties. The others scattered, but Smith was hit twice. She suffered injuries to her groin and hip. Her bladder and spleen were damaged and she was unconscious.

The man escaped, but he was later captured and jailed for life. Smith recovered, but she never did operational police work again. She remained in the RCMP and worked in the recruiting branch in British Columbia. The case was studied extensively by the force in an effort to determine what Smith and the other officers did wrong. It turned out they had made several errors, but they all added up to carelessness and complacency. "Hindsight is 20/20," Best told the recruits. "This kind of thing could have happened to anyone, at any time, regardless of how much service they had." She warned them against leaving the Academy and feeling that "the badge is ten feet tall and it's bulletproof. As time passes, you notice how small your badge is. It's dime size, and it won't stop a B.B. The fun and games are over, folks. It's all for real now."

chapter seven

"I wanted to feel the maximum pain to get ready for the street."

Dave Attew was a muscular charmer with an impish grin. He was six-foot-two and weighed 220 pounds, and had been a bouncer in a bar before joining the Mounties. He liked to go out drinking, and knew how to have a good time. His troopmates nicknamed him Zsa Zsa because of his elegant tastes. He kept a silk comforter in his locker, and liked to get out of his uniform and into his expensive preppie clothes. He joked about his unusual last name, saying that most people mistakenly put the accent on the first syllable. "It's not AT-tew," he said. "It's At-TEW. I'm just a God-damned sneeze."

He had a reputation among his troopmates as a party animal and a ladies' man. It was easy to see where he got it one Saturday afternoon in mid-February, as he snuggled up to an attractive young woman in a downtown Regina hotel room. Patricia Meyer was tall, slim and sexy. She had flown in from Vancouver to spend the Valentine's weekend with Attew, and had decorated the twelfth-floor room in the Ramada Renaissance, Regina's swankiest hotel, with pink balloons and red hearts.

Meyer sat close beside him on the bed as he talked about the rigors of training and the way he relieved the pressure from time to time. He said that going out drinking helped him wind down and keep his sanity. "You just have to get out to relax," he said. "It's just the boys having a good time. I maybe have the odd dance with a girl, but there's nothing to it."

That drew a pout from Meyer, who didn't like the idea of her boyfriend in the arms of another woman, even if it was just an innocent dance. Attew picked up on her displeasure right away, and quickly added, "At the end of the evening I go home with the guys. It's more of a stress release, getting away from Depot and being around normal people."

He denied rumors that he was a womanizer, and said it was just part of the act he liked to put on when he was clowning around. He liked to play the part of the fool and the macho man, but really he was a sensitive guy. But he admitted his reputation as a partier had some basis in fact. On weekends, he said, he and some other members of the troop liked to live it up. One weekend one of them passed out in a bathtub, and another time, "a couple of the boys had to be carried back up to the dorm, and we obtained the reputation of going out and partying all the time."

At twenty-two, Attew was one of the younger members of Troop 17, and he was certainly one of the most fun-loving. He said he was that way by nature, and that he had been advised before coming to the Academy that he would be wise not to take anything too seriously. He had met a lot of Mounties when he worked as a bouncer, and they had told him that at Depot, "they just see how far they can push you. Don't take things personally. If you do, you're going to be one of the people who lets everything build up inside, and you're going to explode, or become an alcoholic."

Attew enjoyed life, but he had his serious side. He was a poor swimmer when he started training, but he worked at it and gained a fair degree of proficiency in the pool. He also knew how to come through when the chips were down. When he did badly on his first-aid exam, he studied intensely and got a near-perfect score on his next test, bringing his average up to a passing level. He joked about being a jock, but he was a serious athlete. Before joining the force he played in the Western Hockey League, just one step down from the NHL. He played on the Academy's hockey team, and put in many extra hours practising and going to games. Sometimes he didn't get back from out-of-town matches until 4 a.m., and had to be in class by eight. During breaks between classes, he sometimes put his head down on the desk and caught a few minute's sleep.

Attew joined the RCMP instead of a city police force because he had found that city cops often had "negative attitudes" and didn't take pride in their work. He thought of the Mounties as an "elite outfit," and wanted to be part of the best. He hoped to be sent to a large detachment "where there's a lot of crime and a lot of excitement. I don't want to sit around in the car eating doughnuts. I want to be in a place where I can learn as much as possible."

Attew was also serious about Patricia Meyer. She worked as a claims assistant in an insurance brokerage in downtown Vancouver. She met Attew in a bar about a month after he moved to British Columbia from Edmonton, where he grew up. They had been going out

Dave Attew and Patricia Meyer spend Valentine's weekend together.

for a couple of years, and she wore his ring on the third finger of her left hand. She described it as a "promise ring." After graduation, they were going to try living together, to see how they got along and give her a chance to find out what life would be like married to a Mountie.

Attew had gone through a lot to have this special weekend with his girlfriend. Earlier in the week, he had been sent to the hospital with severe pain in his abdomen. An appendix operation was scheduled, but when the pain subsided Attew persuaded the doctor to call off the surgery and release him from the hospital.

But then he was confined to the barracks for the weekend because he was caught with some of his homework not done. He got out of that one by going to the sergeant major and pleading with him. The SM had no sympathy for the plight of the young lovers, but Attew found the way to the sergeant major's heart. He said Meyer had a non-refundable air ticket and couldn't reschedule her visit. Several hundred dollars were at stake. The sergeant major was known to be a reasonable man when it came to that sort of thing. "After much yelling, he agreed to let me serve my time the following weekend."

But there was yet one more hitch. It was almost as if that weekend was cursed. Troop 17 was hit with a stand-to inspection for having a dirty dormitory, which meant that they all had to stay in the dorm on Friday night. Attew had planned to pick Meyer up at the airport right after classes ended, but because of the stand-to, he couldn't leave the base. Meyer waited in the hotel room while Attew and the rest of the troop got themselves and their dorm ready for inspection.

When the troop failed the first time around and a second stand-to was ordered for later that night, Attew decided that enough was enough. He hadn't seen Meyer since Christmas. Now she was just a couple of miles away, eagerly awaiting his arrival. He was damned if he was going to sit around shining his boots.

He talked his way out of the second stand-to by shading the truth just a little. He said the sergeant major had given him permission to leave the base for the weekend, neglecting to mention that the special permission had been granted to cover his confinement to the base for not having his homework done. It didn't extend to the mandatory inspections and stand-tos. But dropping the sergeant major's name did the trick, and Attew got permission to leave.

While the rest of the troop grumbled and got ready for the second stand-to, Attew was on his way to the Ramada Renaissance. He had a wonderful weekend with Meyer, and the sergeant major never found out about the small role he played in helping to make it possible.

Joe Kohut was also involved with a beautiful woman, but he didn't have to pack all his loving into one weekend. Kohut brought his fiancée, Marilyn Frederiksen, back to Regina with him after the Christmas break. They shared an apartment and spent as much time as they could together.

Frederiksen had wanted to come to Regina with Kohut when he started training in October, but he wouldn't let her. He told her he was going to be busy day and night for the first three months, and he feared that having her nearby would distract him from his work. "I knew it was going to be hectic, and I figured I wouldn't have much time to see her," he explained.

But he did pretty well at the Academy, and decided that bringing his fiancée to Regina might not be such a bad idea. He went out to look at apartments a couple of weeks before Christmas, and found a place about two miles from the Academy which rented on a month-by-month basis. He went home to Winnipeg at Christmas and gave her the good news. Frederiksen moved in after the holidays, and two weeks later Troop 17 moved up to "senior troop" status. That meant the recruits no longer had to be back on the base by 10:30 p.m. on weeknights and were limited to only one weekend pass a month. Seniors could stay out each weeknight until 1:30, and could leave the base every weekend. Kohut took advantage of his new freedom to go to the apartment as often as he could. Many of his troopmates were jealous. They were stuck in the dorm with a bunch of guys, while Kohut was in a comfortable apartment with his sweetie.

Frederiksen was twenty-three, a year older than Kohut. She was a tall blonde farm girl who left home when she was seventeen. She met Kohut while she was working in a restaurant in Winnipeg and he was a high school student. "I happened to give him my phone number," she recalled, "but we never got together at that time. He went his way, and I went mine."

Joe Kohut and Marilyn Frederiksen share an evening at their apartment in downtown Regina. Kohut was engaged to Frederiksen, but, at least until he finished training, he was married to the RCMP.

Kohut went to community college in The Pas, Manitoba, and took a course in natural resources management while Frederiksen continued to work in Winnipeg. A couple of years after their first encounter, they met by chance again in a bar. "He remembered my face, but I couldn't remember who he was," she recalled. "We started going out, and just kind of fell in love." They were planning to get married the following year.

She was looking forward to being a Mountie's wife. She liked the idea of living in different parts of the country. "I was sick of living in Winnipeg and I wanted to get out and see the world," she said. But she wasn't crazy about Regina, either, and she was looking forward to leaving and going with Kohut to his first detachment. She didn't have any friends in Regina, and took a job as a waitress to help pass the time. Kohut was gone all day, and often he was also busy at night.

Having his fiancée nearby was nice, but he still had plenty of work to do, even if he was in the second half of his training. He felt he had to give the Academy top priority, and Frederiksen would have to play second fiddle. He was a conscientious recruit. Some people in the troop felt that he was almost too keen, and that he sometimes got carried away, especially in self-defence class.

"Sometimes I went 100 percent," he admitted. A lot of the others held back, not wanting to be too hard on themselves and their troopmates, but Kohut gave it all he had. "I wanted to feel the maximum pain, to get ready for the street." A few eyebrows were raised when Kohut seemed to go too far when he was ground fighting with Lorin Lopetinsky. "He [Lopetinsky] had a bandaged leg and told me to take it easy, but when we sparred he came at me, and on instinct I responded. He went down and was rolling around on the floor yelling. I didn't go after him that hard, but it was tender."

After that, he tried to be more careful. "I didn't want to be known as Mr. Aggressive," he said. Frederiksen didn't see him that way at all. She described him as "really sweet, a real tough guy in public, but with me he's a real sensitive guy."

Kohut usually didn't arrive at the apartment until late in the evening, and even then he often had work to do. He would bring his books with him and study, or sit with Frederiksen on the couch and shine his boots. She didn't mind watching TV while he worked, but sometimes it was lonely. She spent a lot of hours waiting for him to come to the poorly-lit basement apartment, which they rented for $285 a month. Kohut had wanted to get a nicer place on a upper floor, but Marilyn had insisted on bringing her cat along, and the landlord wouldn't allow pets in the upper floors. The cat kept her company while she waited for Kohut.

Frederiksen had been excited when Kohut started at the Academy. She got caught up in his enthusiasm for the RCMP, but by the time she had been with him in Regina for a couple of months, the novelty had worn off. "I get sick of hearing RCMP this, RCMP that," she complained. "When we go home and he talks to my mum and dad, that's all you hear. Then we go to his house, and that's still all you hear. Everybody wants to know how it's going for Joe. I hear the same stories five times over."

She couldn't even get away from it when they went for a drive. One of Kohut's duties was to spot at least one infraction every day and record the details in his police notebook. While out for a drive, Frederiksen would want to talk about anything but the RCMP, but Kohut would spot an illegal left turn or some other offence, and out came the notebook. He was engaged to Marilyn Frederiksen, but, at least until he finished training, he was married to the RCMP.

One day Maureen Jones came to the Academy to talk to the recruits about battered women and sexual assault. She caught their attention by asking for volunteers to come to the front of the classroom and answer questions about their sex lives. "I'm going to ask you to discuss some of the most intimate details," Jones informed them. "I may ask about your first sexual experience, or your most recent one. I want you to talk for about two minutes, and then I'll ask more questions. Who wants to volunteer?"

Recruits during Maureen Jones' lecture on sexual assault.

Nobody did. She picked up the attendance clipboard and chose four names at random. The recruits she chose smiled nervously and looked down at the floor. There was a lot of joking about sex at the Academy, and they hoped Jones wasn't serious. But she insisted they come to the front of the room, and when they got there she wondered out loud which one she should start with. She dragged it out, giving them plenty of time to become quite uncomfortable. Then she picked Jason Kerr, the youngest member of the troop. He was only twenty, and he didn't look like he had much sexual experience. Jones paused, looked Kerr in the eye, and told him and the others they could go and sit down. They were off the hook.

Jones was the executive director of the Saskatoon Sexual Assault Centre. She said she wanted to give the recruits some idea what it was like for a sexual assault victim to have to provide details to police officers and other strangers. She had known cases in which victims had been questioned on the witness stand for as much as eight hours. She told the recruits that police officers should offer emotional support to a woman who says she has been assaulted. They should tell her they are sorry about what has happened to her, and reassure her that she is not alone. They should tell her about shelters and other places where she can get help, and explain the procedures involved when criminal charges are laid against the assailant.

Jones also gave the recruits advice on what they should not do. They shouldn't offer coffee to someone who has been forced to perform oral sex until after she has been medically examined, and they shouldn't call the offender a pervert or other derogatory names. "This could elicit defensive reactions from the victim," Jones pointed out. "The man who assaulted her may also have taken her fishing. But don't call him a gentleman either, elevating him in status. Use neutral language, and be non-judgmental."

She finished the class with some role-playing. Jones pretended to be a sleazy woman with a criminal record who said she had been called a slut by her friends for going into the bedroom with the drunken man who victimized her. It would have been easy to be unsympathetic, but the recruits treated her with respect and comforted her. Jones said they were on the right track.

A few days later, another guest lecturer talked to the class. Norm Wilson was a retired Mountie and a recovering alcoholic. He came to warn the recruits that the stress of police work made them especially vulnerable to the dangers of drinking too much.

Wilson said the first time he realized he had a serious problem, he was at the Academy. At that time he had eighteen years of service, and the last thing he remembered was being in Swift Current, about 150 miles west of Regina, picking up three other Mounties who were going to the Academy with him for a refresher course. The next thing he knew, he woke up in a strange bed. He didn't know where he was, or even what day it was. It turned out to be Monday, and he was in one of the dormitories. He had "lost" almost a complete day. "I was scared, really scared," he told the recruits. "I had no idea what had happened for all those hours. I could have held up a 7-Eleven store, raped somebody, shot somebody." He sat in a stairwell and wept for half an hour. Then he telephoned a friend, who took him to a doctor. That's how Norm Wilson, veteran Mountie and veteran lush, started to come to grips with the fact that he was an alcoholic.

"I had suffered a blackout," he said. After he got to Regina, he learned, he had gone drinking with his friends, and late that Sunday night he had crawled into a bed in one of the dorms. He had tied one on, which was nothing unusual for Norm Wilson, but the blackout affected him profoundly. "I was more afraid than when I faced a guy with a double-barrelled shotgun," he remembered. "Alcoholics won't quit drinking until they're damn good and ready, and that day I was ready." He went home and sought help by going to an Alcoholics Anonymous meeting in the small Saskatchewan town where he was posted. He was surprised to meet a lot of people he knew. "The mayor was there, and the Crown attorney, and the judge, and a couple of defence counsels and some rich farmers. It turned out a lot of other people had the same problem I did."

Wilson soon started trying to help other Mounties with booze problems. At first, he said, he encountered a lot of official resistance. The force didn't want to admit that it had drunks in its ranks, and some of the higher-ups weren't interested in helping alcoholic members. Wilson said they would transfer them to remote locations or "put them on highway patrol so they would have an accident and could be fired for drinking and driving."

Wilson speaks with the troop about the dangers of alcohol. "Alcoholics don't quit drinking until they're damned good and ready, and that day I was ready."

Wilson himself had been handled that way a few years before he quit drinking. "The officer in command told me I was a drunk. He punished me by putting me on highway patrol." He recalled sitting in a cruiser in the median of a highway, watching traffic go by while he polished off a forty-ounce bottle of liquor.

Wilson said the force had changed its policy since the days when he was drinking. "A member today probably couldn't get away with drinking a lot for as long as I did. Today the force wouldn't tolerate it. You would be confronted and told to get some help."

He asked how many of the members of the troop were drinkers. All but one of them said they used alcohol. The only abstainer was Jason Kerr, who grew up in a home where liquor was banned for religious reasons. About half the troop said they drank heavily sometimes. Wilson said he wasn't going to try and make them feel guilty about it. He joked about the days "when my head hurt so much I could hear my hair grow, and when I was down on the floor in the bathroom with my arms wrapped around the big white throne."

But then he got serious and urged them to drink responsibly, and to watch for signs that they might be getting into trouble with alcohol. He estimated that fifteen percent of the members of the force were alcoholics, compared with ten percent of the general population. "Take it from an old dumb sergeant like me," he said. "Help is available, and you should get help if you need it."

One of the ways the recruits learned how to do police work was by taking part in "scenarios." These were simulations in which the instructors or fellow-recruits played the parts of citizens with an assortment of complaints and problems. Near the end of training, professional actors were brought in to add a note of realism. Sometimes the recruits had to deal with fairly simple and peaceful matters, and sometimes they got into violent confrontations with people who had guns and knives. Like working police officers, they never knew what they were going to run up against.

One of their first scenarios began with a complaint from Mrs. Green about a noisy mid-afternoon party next door. Wayne Gallant and Lorin Lopetinsky, armed with revolvers which had been welded shut for training purposes, took the call. They knocked on the door and were greeted by two men who looked like construction workers. They were drinking beer and their radio was blaring rock music. One of the men invited the police officers inside.

That put Gallant and Lopetinsky on the spot. Should they walk into this unknown situation? These tough-looking guys might start a fight. They might even try to kill them. Should the young Mounties draw their guns? The two recruits knew that using that kind of force would be out of line. They had been taught to use only as much force as was necessary. But they had also been told not to be foolhardy. Smart cops didn't walk into any situation without anticipating that something dangerous could happen. The best thing to do was to go inside, stay alert for any sign of trouble, and keep their hands free in case they needed to react quickly.

That's how Gallant and Lopetinsky played it. They politely asked the two men to turn down their radio. The men wanted to know who had complained about their party. The recruits again acted correctly. They declined to reveal the complainant's identity. They were friendly but firm. The two men responded well to this approach, promising to keep the noise down.

The two "beer drinkers" were Corporal Glenn Miller, Troop 17's human relations instructor, and Corporal Perry Kuzma, another teacher. The scene was played out in a trailer equipped with cameras and microphones. Nearby, in a second trailer, the rest of the troop watched on a big television screen. The scenario was recorded so the recruits who took part could review their performance later.

Gallant and Lopetinsky did well. They had used good human relations skills and had not overreacted, but their instructors told them that they should have been more careful. They should have obtained more information before walking into the unknown situation. For instance, they should have asked the dispatcher if there had been any previous trouble calls at that address. They should also have peeked in a window before knocking on the door, to get an idea of what was waiting for them inside. They should also have stood to the side when they knocked on the door so they wouldn't be in the line of fire in case somebody with a gun opened the door.

Lorin Lopetinsky tries to mediate a rapidly escalating argument as actor Leslie Mair screams at him to do his job. The actors bring a new level of emotion and realism to the recruits' training.

Keith Blake tries to calm a distraught Chris Cunningham. Scenario topics could vary from domestic disputes, to rape or murder, to announcing the sudden death of a child. The unpredictable nature and intensity of these final scenarios often threw the recruits off balance.

The same scenario was played out again a few minutes later with John Babbitt and Bob Fremlin, who had been sent out of the viewing room and had not seen what happened to the first two recruits. This time the "drinkers" were less co-operative. Miller demanded to know what the cops were going to do if he refused to turn down the radio. Babbitt and Fremlin were unsure of themselves. They didn't know if there was a law against making excessive noise in the afternoon.

Then the sound of a police siren came though the window. It was from another training exercise nearby, but Kuzma picked up on it and started to look around nervously, as if he were frightened. He got up suddenly and started to walk down the hall. The recruits took this as a potential threat to their safety. Was Kuzma going to get a gun? Should they arrest him? On what grounds? Fremlin started to go after Kuzma. Miller started yelling and demanded that the police officers get out of his house. The situation was starting to get out of control, and that's where the instructors brought the scenario to an end.

Back in the classroom, they went over the events and showed the recruits how they could have handled the situation more effectively. They pointed out that police officers who looked like they didn't know the law commanded little respect. They also told the recruits that they had to respect citizens' rights, and look at things from the public's point of view. How would they feel if they were having an innocent little afternoon drinking party and the cops treated them like criminals? How would they feel if they started to walk toward the washroom, and a police officer came chasing after them?

The recruits learned that there were no pat answers. Each situation was different, and there were a lot of factors to be considered. They had to learn the difference between being careful and being paranoid. They had to be firm but not throw their weight around. The scenarios gave them experience, and they learned from their mistakes.

❖ ❖ ❖

The Academy had two classrooms set up like RCMP detachment offices. There was also a jail cell and a courtroom. These were used near the end of Troop 17's training, when the recruits took part in scenarios which involved going to the scene of a crime, making an arrest, taking the accused back to the office, locking him up, doing the paperwork, and taking the case to court.

One of the scenarios started when Lorin Lopetinsky and Trevor MacKay were in one of the detachment offices and the telephone rang. "Hello, police?" shouted a woman. "I want to report a man in the laundromat trying to sell a gun." Colette Perrier was playing the part of the complainant, and had been instructed to volunteer only a little information. Lopetinsky and MacKay had to ask her a lot of questions to learn as much as possible before going into a potentially violent situation. They spent about ten minutes on the phone with her, and before they left they had learned quite a bit — what the man looked like, what he was wearing, what kind of a gun he had, who else was in the laundromat and so forth.

Armed and ready, Marty Schneider and Pat Zunti respond to a scenario complaint of a man firing shots at an apartment complex.

Marty Schneider leads a suspect, Kerry Mah, back to the detachment to book him.

The scenarios continue in bits and pieces over a few week. The recruits prepare for court and take the witness stand when their case comes to trial.

Corporal Karen Adams from operational training plays the judge for one scenario.

The two officers approached the laundromat cautiously, with their guns drawn. Before going inside, they had taken the precaution of asking the dispatcher for a "ten-minute call-back." If they didn't call back on the radio in ten minutes, the dispatcher would assume they were in trouble and would send help.

The two cops snuck up to the laundromat, peeked inside, poked their guns through the door and got the drop on the "bad guy," Dan Thorne, who was sitting in a chair eating an apple. They ordered him to stand up, handcuffed him and read him his rights. Lopetinsky found a revolver in the pocket of a jacket which was hanging over the back of a nearby chair. Thorne had been told to deny that the gun was his. Dressed in grubby clothes, he looked more like a punk than a recruit, and he put on a convincing performance. He accused the police officers of being "fags" when they searched near his groin. The police officers ignored his insults and discovered a knife in his underwear. They took him back to the detachment and searched him again. They turned up a packet of white powder in his sock.

Lopetinsky and MacKay put the gun, the knife and the drugs in a security locker. Then they took Thorne next door and locked him in a cell. It looked like a good piece of police work, and in many ways it was, but during the critique which followed, errors quickly showed up. What about the ten-minute call-back which they had requested? They had forgotten about it. If it had been a real situation, other police officers would have been pulled from their duties and sent to the laundromat unnecessarily. What about the jacket? Lopetinsky and MacKay had left it in the detachment when they took Thorne next door to the cell. They should have put the jacket in the security locker with the rest of the evidence. It was crucial to the case because it linked Thorne to the gun.

The scenario continued in bits and pieces over the following week, much like a real case that would move through the legal system. MacKay and Lopetinsky filled out paperwork. They prepared the case for court, and got up on the witness stand when it came to trial. Corporals played the parts of the judge and the lawyers. The charge was thrown out. Thorne was accused of being in possession of an unregistered firearm, but Lopetinsky and MacKay had failed to run a computer check on the gun, and had no evidence that the weapon was

unregistered. The cops had blown it. Thorne played his part right to the end, smirking as he breezed past the crestfallen rookies, who learned that if they were going to be successful in their work, they had to get everything right.

That was the thing about Depot. No matter how good you were, and no matter how hard you tried, it was impossible to get everything right. That's the way the place was set up. Failure was part of the game. It was all right to blow it once in awhile, as long as you learned from your mistakes. Even the best recruits sometimes failed. They got another chance, and usually they got it right the second time around. That's what happened to John Christensen.

At six-foot-five and 235 pounds, Christensen was not only the biggest man in the troop, he was also one of the best. He was twenty-seven years old and had grown up in the RCMP. His father, Murray Christensen, had risen through the ranks and had become a commissioned officer. He retired as a superintendent, and had passed on his love of police work and pride in the force to his son.

Christensen had several other things going for him. He had a friendly, easy-going manner. He had six years of university and held degrees in arts and education. He taught school and worked in public relations before joining the Mounties, and his communications skills were strong. He became bilingual during eight months of language training in Montreal before he went to the Academy.

Christensen was a bright light, and right from the start he stood out as one of the top recruits. But inevitably, he soon got into trouble. It happened in the drill hall, right after the troop had been in self-defence class. "Everybody's elbows were bleeding because we had to get down and crawl across the mats. I was on the end and Corporal Ferguson came up to me and looked at my elbows and saw just a little bit of blood. He yelled at me for having blood on my uniform and asked me why. I explained it, and he gave me five days of early morning remedial parade. At the same time, Constable Tyreman, who stood beside me, had both of his buttons on his shirt undone, and Constable Polk, who was four people away from me, had so much blood on his elbows that he looked like he had been in a car accident. Those two people were skipped over completely."

Such was justice in the drill hall. Christensen thought it was unfair, but he wasn't surprised that it happened. He had heard from his father and his older brother Jim, who was also a Mountie, that this sort of thing was bound to happen at some point in his training. "You are going to feel that you are being mistreated, or unjustly treated," he had been told. "It's part of the game. It's teaching you to put up with the Mickey Mouse things in life, and you have to learn not to worry about them."

Christensen had a good role model. His father was an easy-going policeman who said he had never had to wrestle a person he had arrested into a jail cell. He found that he was much better off talking to the person. He had gone through the Academy in 1948, and had noted a lot of changes by the time his son was in training. There were no human relations classes or training scenarios then, and a lot of what John was being taught at the Academy had to be learned on the job in Murray Christensen's day.

"Our training wasn't as complete as it is today," he said. "There was more emphasis on the physical aspects of training. Police-community relations was almost non-existent. We had boys from Toronto or Montreal who finished training and were sent out to Manitoba or Saskatchewan. They would be stationed at small detachments near native populations, and they had no experience or training in this area. It took a little while for a young chap to get into the system and to come to the point where he could not only have patience with the

While waiting for Corporal Ferguson's arrival, John Christensen playfully provides Keith Blake with a set of rabbit ears during early morning parade. Christensen's easy going manner helped him get along with all kinds of people.

people he dealt with, but patience with himself. He needed to have patience with other people's impatience."

When Murray was in training, the recruits spent a lot of time on menial tasks which did little to prepare them for police work. A lot of the things they did revolved around horses. The Academy was far behind the times, continuing to emphasize horses when most police officers were riding around in cars.

"We had to work in the stables before breakfast, and we had stables again in the evenings," Murray recalled. "We also often stood night guard, which meant we were in charge of the guard room until eight the next morning. Then you slept in until eleven, and then you were up and you had to go to class. You were a little bleary-eyed during that afternoon."

That was one thing that hadn't changed over the years. The recruits in Troop 17 often got too little sleep, and that was a big factor when John Christensen got into trouble again near the end of training. This time it was in driver training class, and the potential price of failure was much higher than the five days he spent on bozo parade for having bloody elbows.

Driver training was a key part of the Academy's program. The typical RCMP officer spent about sixty percent of his time in a cruiser, and the driver training section had more instructors than any other unit. One instructor usually went out in a car for three hours with two recruits, so they got plenty of driving practice. The instructor critiqued their performance as they went along.

The program emphasized defensive driving skills, and also included things like overtaking cars and making emergency turns. Troop 17 had two cars available after hours, and the recruits spent a lot of time practising their skills by driving around the streets of Regina in the evenings and on weekends.

Their driving performance was tested several times as they moved through training, and Christensen did well until the end. The final test was known as Drive 10, because it was the tenth and last in the sequence. It was the hardest of them all. A recruit who failed Drive 10 was given a second chance, five days after his first attempt. If he failed again, he was held back and given individual instruction for two weeks, while his troopmates went to their first detachments.

The recruit would go through the graduation ceremony with the others, but it would be a "dummy graduation." No public announcement would be made, but the commanding officer would hand him an empty badge pouch. He wouldn't get his badge until he put in the extra two weeks and passed Drive 10. It would be a serious blow to the recruit's morale and pride, and in Christensen's case it would have been especially difficult. The sons of RCMP members or retired Mounties who had risen above the rank of constable could have their badges presented to them by their fathers. It was one of the traditions of the force, one of the ways a veteran Mountie could "pass the torch" to his son. But it wouldn't happen if Christensen didn't pass Drive 10.

"It was a bad day," he recalled. "We had our two-hour human relations exam first thing in the morning. It's one of the exams that has a reputation for screwing people up in the last couple of weeks of training, so people study a lot for it. I got only about two hours sleep the night before. I wrote the exam in the morning and had Drive 10 in the afternoon."

The test required him to go through downtown Regina, and that's where he got into trouble. "It was my fault. I got caught for driving through an intersection when a pedestrian was about to cross in front of me. She had started crossing in one direction, and then changed her direction. I failed to see her change in mid-stream, so by the rules, I failed."

Christensen didn't let the failure throw him. He had done well on all of his previous drives, and felt that he just got a bad break on the last one. "Talking with a lot of people, I found that it happens sometimes. It's the odds. Sooner or later, your number is going to come up. It didn't diminish my confidence whatsoever. At one particular time and in one set of circumstances, I made a mistake. It could have gone the same way for anybody else."

Five days later, he took the exam again. He passed the test easily. He did so well that the instructor complimented him on his performance. "There were no other exams going on, so there was no pressure. I was relaxed, and everything went great." He called his father and told him there was going to be a badge in the leather pouch on graduation day.

✣ ✣ ✣

John Christensen receives his badge from his father, Superintendent Murray Christensen (retired), as Chief Superintendent William Spring, looks on.

chapter eight

"We accomplished the impossible."

Chief Superintendent William R. Spring, the officer in charge of the Academy, was just three ranks down from the top of the force. Of the 20,000 or so members of the RCMP, only eighteen assistant commissioners, four deputy commissioners and the commissioner himself, Norman Inkster, outranked him. As the OIC of the Academy, Spring was right up there in the Mountie hierarchy, but he knew what it was like to be on the bottom. He started his career as a recruit at the Training Academy, just like every other Mountie. Unlike the Armed Forces, the RCMP does not have a special entry system for commissioned officers. There are no "shave-tail" officers in the RCMP. Every Mountie who wins a commission is a veteran who has worked his way up through the ranks, and has usually been a member of the force for at least fifteen years.

Spring was just nineteen when he joined the RCMP in 1960. He was an impetuous kid who dropped out of high school only a month before he was scheduled to graduate. He signed up in Calgary one Saturday, hopped on a train to Regina, and leapt into training the following Monday morning. He enjoyed being a recruit, and never dreamed he would someday come back as the OIC. "The officers were far removed from me in terms of my career aspirations," he recalled. "I was just thinking about getting through training and then going out and doing some police work."

Constable Spring wasn't big for a police officer. He was a bit under five-foot-ten, and weighed only 159 pounds. There were a lot of bigger recruits in his troop, and several of them had joined the Mounties after serving in the Canadian Forces. Spring had to hustle to keep up with them. "Some days I was pretty beat," he remembered. "We had to get up almost every day, including Saturday, for early parade at 6:15. Then we had jobs to do, like sweeping, shovelling snow, cutting grass, weeding, taking care of the horses and cleaning the stables, before we had breakfast." Then there were classes all day, and more routine jobs to do each night. The idea was to keep the recruits busy, "but it was a lot of fun," Spring said, "and I enjoyed it."

Veteran members of the force often said that recruits were better and training was harder in the old days, but Spring didn't see things that way. "You can delude yourself by thinking that, but today's recruits are more committed. Some have waited five or eight years or even longer to get in here. The laws are more complex, and the academic aspect is far heavier than when I went through. When I was a recruit, the only reason I would've been on the base on a Friday or Saturday night or Sunday was because I was CBed, not because I was studying or practising driving or doing any of the things that I see the recruits doing today. Nobody is telling them that they must do it, but they are committed to what they are doing, and they spend much of their spare time working. We spent our spare time going to movies or dances or the bar."

Horsemanship was part of the training program when Spring was a trainee, and the program was nine months long to provide time for equitation classes. The recruits spent many hours learning how to ride, and then they got a lot of cavalry drill. Many of the old routines have been preserved in the world-famous RCMP Musical Ride. The recruits in Spring's day played games to improve their riding skills. One of them involved bringing the horse to a gallop, lowering a lance to the attack position, spearing a tent peg which had been stuck in the ground, and carrying the peg on the tip of the lance to the end of the course. The recruits also played a game which was something like soccer on horseback. They manoeuvered their mounts so that the animals' legs and withers push a large air-filled leather ball through a set of goal posts. Then there was the Balaklava Melee. Teams of riders wore helmets which were like fencing masks, with a feather loosely attached to the top. The idea was to knock the opponent's feather off with a four-foot bamboo truncheon. The recruits often got whacked on their unprotected arms, hands and shoulders.

As head of the RCMP Training Academy, Spring has one of the most highly visible positions in the RCMP. He oversees an academy with an annual budget of $35 million and about 600 recruits at the time Troop 17 was in training.

Riding could be a rough business, as young Spring found out one day when he was in the arena on the back of a horse named Imp. "It was a small horse, but quite feisty," he recalled. "I had ridden a bit before joining the mounted police, but I was used to a western saddle, and they used the English saddle. We were in the arena doing our movements, and I guess I touched the horse with my spurs and at the same time pulled the reins. Imp started bucking and went forwards and backwards. I stayed on for a little while, but finally I went over the back of the horse and was hit by both hind legs while I was in the air. He gave me a good shot."

The riding master told Spring that if he couldn't ride, he should get out of the arena. He dragged himself into the tack room, lay down on a table, and somebody called an ambulance. He had several broken ribs and an injured kidney, and spent a month in the hospital. He was backtrooped when he got back to Depot, but he fit in well with the new group of recruits, and graduated second in his class.

He spent the early part of his career in British Columbia. For the first year or so, he was a "goofy young guy who was out to change the world and make everybody right." He got into trouble once for drinking under age at a party. Somebody complained to his detachment commander and the twenty-year-old Spring was reprimanded and transferred to Kamloops. That's where a tragic incident made him start taking life more seriously. Another Mountie who was supposed to work Sunday night asked Spring to trade shifts with him, and he agreed. The next day, when Spring had originally been scheduled to work, the other Mountie was working in Spring's place. A call came into the detachment office about a man with a gun who was making threats at the welfare office. When the police arrived, he opened fire. The Mountie who had traded shifts with Spring was killed, along with two other police officers.

The tragedy made him realize that police work was a deadly serious business, and "I decided to get serious about my career." He spent about seven years in detachment policing and then moved into administration. He was promoted to corporal and then to sergeant, and along the way he earned a community college diploma in business administration and a university degree in psychology and sociology. He was commissioned at the age of thirty-six and worked at various posts in Ottawa before being assigned to the RCMP's official languages directorate. When the top job in the directorate opened up, Spring was appointed to it and made a big career move. He leap-frogged over the rank of superintendent, jumping from inspector to chief superintendent. He was on the fast track in the upper echelons of the mounted police. He soon became deputy director of personnel in Ottawa, and then spent a year at the National Defence College in Kingston and travelled to more than twenty-five countries on an international study program before taking command of the Academy in 1989.

It was a big job. The Academy was one of the showplaces of the RCMP, and Spring had one of the most highly visible positions in the force. It was also a big business operation, with an annual budget of about $35 million and about 600 recruits on the base at various levels of training while Troop 17 was there. The academy was cranking out so many Mounties that Spring sometimes thought of it as a giant automobile factory. He compared the recruits to

Buicks moving down the assembly line, being built for the Academy's "customers" across the land. The customers included the force itself, the eight provinces (all except Ontario and Quebec) which had contracts with the RCMP to provide provincial policing, and the 175 cities and towns which had contracts with the force for municipal police service.

Spring had high standards. He wouldn't send out a "Buick" until he was satisfied that it was ready to go in all respects. If the recruit didn't pass every test and meet every behavioral objective that was required of him, he didn't graduate. Spring recalled one case in which a recruit refused to go through the Academy's gas training room. Each trainee was required to remove his gas mask for a few seconds and then put it back on while the room was filled with tear gas. This would give him first-hand experience with the effects of the gas, and teach him how to respond if his mask should get ripped off in a riot.

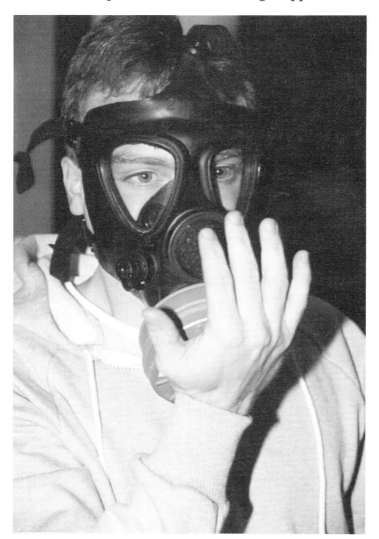

Keith Blake checks his mask before entering the gas chamber. The feeling among the recruits could best be described as grim determination.

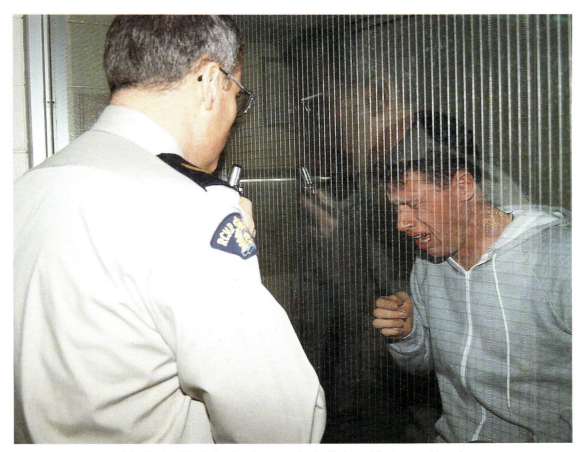

Brian Davison fights for breath in the tear gas chamber. Each recruit has to remove his mask, answer a few simple questions, replace his mask and then is allowed to head outside to fresh air.

Most recruits went through the unpleasant experience with minor discomfort. They had runny eyes and coughed for a few minutes, and then they were fine. But Spring said this particular recruit had a extreme fear of tear gas, and said she would rather fail than go through the gas chamber. It would have meant the end of her career, but her record showed that she was otherwise an excellent recruit, and Spring felt it would be a shame to lose her. So he ordered a special test for her, and arranged for a doctor to be present to assure her that she would get instant medical attention if she should need it. The nervous recruit went into the gas chamber, took off her mask, put it back on, and recovered within a few minutes. She went on to graduate, and Spring was able to send another "Buick" out to one of his "customers."

Chief Superintendent Spring inspected all the troops after they had been at the Academy for about five months, and since there were so many troops, he was doing it almost every week. It was a routine part of his job, but he knew it was special for each of the troops he visited, and he seemed to enjoy it. By that point in their training, Troop 17 had been inspected by corporals and sergeants dozens of times, but the OIC's visit was a big occasion, and they took extra pains to be ready. Failing to win his approval would be a tremendous loss of face for the troop, and by that point Troop 17 had acquired a pretty good reputation around the place. They intended to keep it.

"I worked all week to get ready," said Dave Tyreman, one of the top recruits in the troop. "I spent many, many hours polishing my boots and the leatherwork on my Sam Browne. That bathroom was spotless. We all worked much harder for this than we did for a stand-to. If you fail your OIC's inspection, look out! The weeks you've got remaining here would be miserable. I imagine you'd have 'attitude adjustment' in self-defence, and 'attitude adjustment' in PT, and 'attitude adjustment' in practically everything else. You'd really get run through the ringer."

Spring arrived at 8 a.m. on a Friday morning, accompanied by Sergeant Major Yvon Mercier. The SM barked and the recruits sprang to attention. They were lined up along the aisle in front of their beds. Spring started working his way down the line, while Mercier poked around in the cupboards, examined the recruits' kits and rattled the venetian blinds to see if there was any dust on them. Spring took his time. He spoke with each recruit, asking them about various parts of their training and tossing out quick questions on the law, RCMP regulations and so forth. When he got to the pit shared by Keith Blake and John Christensen, he set up a little scenario. The OIC told the two recruits to assume he was a man walking along the street, and then he dropped a small silver throwing star which he had been carrying in his pocket. Christensen promptly grabbed the OIC's arm, and Blake told him he was under arrest for possession of a restricted weapon. Spring demanded to know what section of the Criminal Code he was being arrested under. The recruits didn't know. He told them to brush up on their law, and moved down the line.

When he got to Dave Dubnyk and Brian Davison, he asked if they were willing to gamble on whether they knew their communications codes. Losing the bet would mean confinement to the base for the upcoming weekend. Dubnyk and Davison confidently agreed to the challenge. "What's a 10-62?" Spring asked. "It means there is an unauthorized listener," Dubnyk correctly responded. Spring asked what the code was when a police officer needed help fast. "10-33," Davison replied. "That's right," Spring said. "I guess you're free for the weekend."

He moved along, and told Bob Fremlin and Mark Gagnier to assume they had received a report that a man had just shoplifted a cassette tape from a record store. He told them to imagine he was a businessman walking down the street, and he pulled a cassette from his pocket. Fremlin and Gagnier politely asked the "businessman" if they could examine the tape he was carrying. When he asked them what this was all about, they explained the situation and won his co-operation. The tape turned out to be dictation the innocent "businessman" was taking to the secretarial service down the street. Spring said that when he pulled the same trick while inspecting another troop the previous week, the recruits were too quick to jump to the wrong conclusion. "They arrested me, and I sued them."

When he got to the end of the dorm, Spring paused while the sergeant major made a quick check of the washroom. It sparkled. Spring nodded and then started working his way back, inspecting the recruits on the opposite side of the aisle. The recruits were wondering what other tricks the commanding officer might have up his sleeve. He casually dropped a packet of white powder on the floor as he passed Dave Rampersad and Aaron Polk. They stopped Spring and questioned him.

The OIC saved his best prop for the last two recruits he inspected, Dave Tyreman and Pat Zunti. He told them to assume they were looking for a man who was wanted for armed robbery. He told them that he matched the description of the suspect, and then slipped into the role. He crouched down, as if he were by the side of a car. The recruits approached cautiously and began to question him. The "suspect" stood up. "Quit bugging me," he said, waving around what appeared to be a silver tire pressure gauge. He pointed it at Zunti and said, "Bang! You're dead!" He revealed that the tire gauge had been hollowed out and rigged with a firing pin so that it could shoot a .22-calibre bullet. "Be a lot more cautious," Spring advised Zunti and Tyreman. "You can see how easily something can happen."

Chief Superintendent Bill Spring inspects Paul Gilligan. Lorin Lopetinsky and Sgt. Major Yvon Mercier look on.

Spring and the sergeant major stepped into the laundry room for a quick consultation. Mercier reported that he had found Troop 17's dorm to be in good shape. He said some of the leather on their Sam Browne belts needed more polishing, and the bands on a couple of their Stetson hats had been put on the wrong way, but otherwise it was "a good turnout." Spring was pleased. He came back into the dorm and the recruits gathered around him as if he were the coach of a winning team. He spoke softly, telling them they had done well and urging them to maintain their high standards. Then he left. As soon as he was out the door, the recruits pranced around like a kennel full of happy puppies, relieved that they had passed. Ron Roberts was especially glad. Somehow he had managed to put his spurs on backwards. Miraculously, neither the OIC nor the sergeant major had noticed.

❖   ❖   ❖

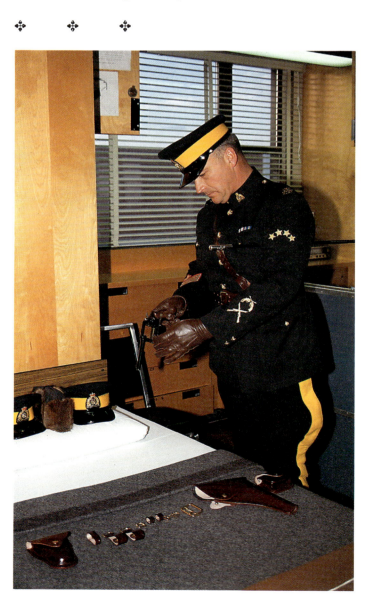

Sgt. Major Yvon Mercier inspects a recruit's kit.
Each piece has to be laid out in an exact way.

The instructors said they could always tell when a troop was about to get its detachment postings. No matter how interesting the lesson was, they had that far-away look. Their minds were in New Brunswick or Alberta or wherever it was that they were going to be sent.

Troop 17's posting process started about halfway through training, when the recruits had their first meeting with a staffing officer. Then each of them was interviewed, and a month later, they were told what province they were going to. In the final few weeks of training, they were given their specific detachment assignments.

Sergeant Michel Lafleur, a personnel specialist, told the recruits that the days were gone when the force sent people wherever it wanted to, with no consideration for their personal circumstances and preferences. "There's no big dart board on the wall," he said. He told them that the force had good reasons for sending people where it did, and that individual situations were taken into account. He told them about one recruit whose son needed surgery. The recruit was posted to a detachment near a major medical centre so the boy could have the operation.

But Lafleur pointed out that in most cases, the "needs of the force" were the prime consideration. He said the RCMP was like a big corporation with branches across the country, and it was routine to transfer staff members to where the company needed them. When recruits complained about where they being sent, he had a stock answer: "When you signed up, you said you'd be willing to serve anywhere in Canada."

Pit partners Mark Skotnicki and Dan Thorne relax after the OIC's Inspection. Some of the troop were dressed in full red serge for the inspection and others were still in brown serge. Members wearing brown had yet to receive their red uniforms from the tailor.

Some of the recruits would have preferred to go back to their home areas, but the force had a policy which prevented that in most cases. The rule was that for the first five years of his career, a Mountie usually did not work in the province where he came from. If he had lived in more than one province, the matter was decided on the basis of where he had spent his "formative years." The purpose of the policy was to give the recruit experience in living in another part of the country, in keeping with the national character of the force, but sometimes the rule was bent if there was an overwhelming personal need for the recruit to go back to his home province, or if for some reason the force needed him there. For instance, he might have language skills that were required in a particular place.

Lafleur gave the recruits a form to fill out on which they were to list the three provinces they would like to be sent to, in their order of preference. He told them to be realistic, and consider their strengths and weaknesses. "If you're a Toronto boy who has seen a picture of a dogsled and always wanted to go to the Arctic, don't expect us to send you there unless you've got something else going for you," he said. "We'll want to know a lot of things about you. Can you get used to three straight months of darkness? Can your wife get used to it? Are you the sort of person who has enough mechanical skill to change a snowmobile spark plug on a trip between settlements? Can you get along where minimum supervision and help are available? If you have any problem with this sort of thing, or any weaknesses at all, you can forget about the North."

Ron Roberts was ecstatic when he got his posting, Charlottetown, P.E.I. A Newfoundland native, he had hoped to remain on the east coast.

Lafleur said, "It would be great if we could please everybody, but you've got to be realistic." He urged the married recruits to talk with their families to see where they wanted to live. He said the wishes of a recruit's spouse and children were important, but little weight would be given to a recruit's desire to be near aging parents. "You knew your mother and father were old when you joined the force."

Lafleur told them that at the moment, there was a big shortage of people in British Columbia, and that's where most of them would likely be sent, but it would depend on circumstances. Things changed very quickly when it came to manpower requirements. "You could all end up going to Ontario or Quebec to provide security against terrorism, depending on how things go in the Gulf War," he told them, but as it happened, the war ended well before they graduated, and most of them wound up being posted to British Columbia, as Lafleur had expected.

Of the thirty recruits, twenty-two went to B.C., mostly to municipal detachments. Three went to Alberta, two to Manitoba, and one each to Ontario, New Brunswick and Prince Edward Island. Happily, the needs of the force meshed with the wishes of most of the recruits. Nineteen of the thirty members of the troop were sent to the province which they ranked first on their list of preferences. Four got their second choice, five got their third choice, and only two were sent to provinces they didn't put on their lists.

One day near the end of training, the recruits had a lesson in ethics. They were shown a video featuring a veteran and a rookie on traffic patrol. The veteran was in trouble for using excessive force the previous week, and he asked his young partner to help him cook up a story to get him off the hook. As he ranted on about how much he hated hippies, a van sped by. The cops gave chase and pulled the van over. The older officer ordered the long-haired male driver to get out of the van, swore at him, pushed him around, handcuffed him and punched him in the stomach. The young cop's face revealed that he didn't like what was happening, but he just stood by and watched. Then a sergeant soon drove up, saw the hippie gasping for breath, eyed the older cop suspiciously, and demanded to know what was going on. The bully glanced furtively at his young partner, expecting him to cover up for him. "Ask Joe," he said. "He saw it all."

The video ended at that point, and the recruits were invited to comment. They criticized the older officer for using excessive force and not controlling his temper. It was easy for them to see that he was in the wrong. The need to control themselves and to use the minimum amount of force necessary to do the job had been drilled into them over and over. But what about Joe? Was he also in the wrong? Should Joe have stepped in when his partner started getting rough? How should Joe answer the sergeant's question? The recruits found these were difficult issues to deal with, and their human relations instructor, Corporal Miller, didn't give them any pat answers. They had to come up with their own solutions.

If they went by the book, their choices were simple. Joe was a peace officer and he should have tried to stop the assault, even if the person committing the assault was his partner. He should have reported it immediately to the sergeant, and he should have given evidence against his partner in an internal RCMP disciplinary hearing or in court if a criminal charge had been laid. But that's not how the recruits saw it.

Some of them said that young Joe should have stepped in when his partner started knocking the driver around, but since he didn't, he should keep his mouth shut. They suggested that Joe could quietly take his partner aside later and tell him that his actions were unacceptable, and that Joe wouldn't cover it up if he did it again. One recruit thought that Joe should go to a more senior officer and tell him "off the record" what happened. Another suggested that Joe should write a detailed report of the incident in his notebook, in case the top brass got involved, or he had to testify about what happened in court.

None of the recruits said that Joe should immediately tell the sergeant that his partner had committed an unprovoked assault on the handcuffed man. None of them said that Joe should volunteer to give evidence against his fellow officer. The recruits felt that Joe had an obligation to be loyal to his partner and to protect him even though the older cop was clearly in the wrong. When one member of the class pointed out that it was a clear case of assault, and that "technically" Joe was obligated to report it, another recruit replied that "technicalities go by the wayside all the time."

Their response wasn't surprising. It was consistent with what they had been taught at the Academy. Loyalty to other members of the force was held out as not only desirable, but essential. The recruits spent months working together and supporting one another. Some of them became so close to others in the troop that they spoke about being willing to "take a bullet" for them, if it should ever come to that. A lot of emphasis was put on "safety first" and "officer survival," and one of the key ways they were taught to protect themselves was by working together and backing each other up. They had been told that when they got out into the field, their partners were going to be their best friends, and that if they wanted to be good Mounties, they had to be team players.

Given all that, it wasn't hard to imagine them closing their eyes or covering up when one of their colleagues stepped out of line. The recruits felt that lying to protect a partner was a smaller sin than telling the truth and selling out a fellow Mountie. But they also revealed that there were limits as to how far they would go. Some said they would feel more obligated to betray a partner if he seriously hurt somebody, but in this case he just pushed the driver around and knocked the wind out of him, so there was not a strong reason to tell the truth. Some felt that while they had a duty to obey the RCMP's motto, which was to "maintiens le droit" (uphold the right), the greater good in this case was to protect the partner.

Self-interest also had to be considered. They knew that snitching on a partner could get a police officer into trouble. Breaking the code of police silence could result in the officer being ostracized by the other officers that he worked with. It could also make him vulnerable to physical danger. He could find himself in a tough spot someday, and his partner wouldn't back him. "If you rat on everybody every time he does something wrong," said one of the recruits, "you're going to be out of luck when it comes to having friends when you need them."

In discussing the case later, Paul Gilligan said he didn't know what he would do if he were in Joe's shoes. "It depends what's inside you," he said. "You have a conflict. One side says you don't want to go against your brother officers, but the other side says that isn't what society is about, that this is not what we're here for. You get into a lot of soul-searching. These are your friends. Are they worth having? If you just turn away, you don't have to get involved, but you have to go to bed that night, and you have to face your family in the morning. You have to go in front of thirty little kids in elementary school who are going to look up to you. I don't think I could do that. If I didn't do something right away, I'd probably quit. I couldn't live with myself."

The hypothetical case was especially interesting because the class dealt with it just a few weeks after a real and highly publicized incident of police brutality in Los Angeles. That case sparked a lot of discussion at the Academy, and several of Troop 17's instructors told the recruits that they were embarrassed to tell people they were police officers, after the way their fellow cops in Los Angeles behaved. The American case involved a black man, Rodney King, who was handcuffed. Four white police officers kicked him, struck him with their batons and jolted him with an electric stun gun. They fractured his eye socket, smashed his cheekbone, broke his leg and caused serious internal injuries. Several other officers stood and watched, or turned their backs while this vicious assault took place. Members of the Los Angeles black community said that such incidents were common, and the only reason this one came to light was that a citizen happened to videotape the beating. It was shown repeatedly on network television, and the eventual acquittal of the officers in court in 1992 led to the Los Angeles riots.

Superintendent Louis Wood didn't get into a long discussion when he spoke to Troop 17 about the Los Angeles case and other incidents of police brutality. Wood said that it was just plain wrong, and told the recruits that the force would not support members who behaved improperly, whether they were actually in on the beating or simply stood back and let it happen. Wood told them that their superior officers expected them to behave ethically, and so did the Canadian public.

Wood was in charge of administration and personnel at the Academy. He said that using excessive force was just one of many things that could get a Mountie into trouble. He told the recruits to keep their noses clean once they got out into the field, and to keep them clean all through their careers. He said that breaking the rules was probably the furthest thing from their minds as they were about to leave the Academy, where the importance of proper behavior had been drummed into them, but he invited them to think ahead ten or fifteen years. By that time, he said, they might have become jaded and the dedication they once had to duty might have diminished. They might be upset because they had been passed over for promotion or posted to an out-of-the-way spot. If that should happen, he suggested, they might be inclined to "start mouthing off."

He warned them not to do that, and urged them to keep their discontent within the "RCMP family." He cautioned them against complaining to outsiders, saying that it would be bad for the force's public image, and it could get them into hot water. "There are certain people who would love to latch on to a disgruntled member," Wood told them. "They'll go after the person who has an axe to grind." He told them they should talk to a trusted friend, a fellow member of the force, the sergeant in charge of their detachment, the force psychologist or the division representative. "Don't keep things bottled up inside, but don't let it come out in a restaurant booth where strangers can overhear you."

Wood said there was big money in things like drugs and prostitution, and warned them against being corrupted by it. "Don't get into debt that you can't handle," he told them. "Don't open yourself up to bribes and blackmail. Watch out for subtle attempts to buy you. Beware of loans which are offered to you at no interest, or at much less than the going rate."

He told them about a Mountie who had an informant who was a prostitute. "One day he ended up in bed with her," Wood said, and that was the start of an illicit sexual relationship which compromised the Mountie's integrity. He was picked up on a surveillance camera other Mounties were using in an investigation, and he lost his job. Wood also told them about a staff sergeant who was living beyond his income and making a lot of trips to South America. One day his luggage was searched, and a large quantity of cocaine was found. He went to jail.

Wood was also Troop 17's "debriefing" officer. Each troop met privately with a senior officer before leaving the Academy. They were invited to level with him and tell him what they really thought of the place. The idea was to give them a chance to complain but to keep it "in the family." It also helped the brass keep tabs on what was going on at the Academy. By listening to the recruits, the officers were able to identify weaknesses in the training system and learn what the recruits thought of their instructors.

If a recruit wanted to suggest an improvement in the way things were done, this was the time to do it. If he wanted to "rat" on an instructor or blow the whistle on a bad situation, he was invited to do that here too. Wood assured them they could speak freely, and promised he wouldn't start digging into problems they disclosed until after they left. That would enable them to speak without fear of retribution from instructors they might wish to complain about.

It was an invitation to let fly with both barrels, but the recruits had no serious complaints. They said they were generally happy with the way they had been trained and thought all of their instructors were okay, and that several of them were very good. But when Wood insisted that there must be some things they felt could be improved, they had quite a few suggestions.

Superintendent Louis Wood and Sergeant Denis Arbez listen to troop complaints at the troop's debriefing.

They wanted more swimming instruction. They said there was too much time spent on exercises like pushups and "ins and outs." This made them fitter, but it didn't teach them to be better swimmers or to be more skilful in saving lives. They wanted more time spent in self-defence classes on skills that would be useful in the field, such as how to use the baton. They felt that there was too much emphasis put on judo, which was fun but wouldn't be much use in a bar fight. They wanted more scenarios. They said some of the material doled out in three-hour lectures could easily be covered in an hour. They felt they could learn more by practising their skills in real-life situations than by sitting around taking notes and regurgitating the information on exams. They also called for more consistency in driver training, saying that they usually had a different instructor every time they went out in the car. One instructor would tell them to do things one way, and the next instructor would tell them to do things another way.

They had a few gripes about what went on outside of classes. They said they often didn't have enough time to eat lunch, especially on days when they had to march in the noon parade. They said that sometimes the portions at supper were too small, especially when chicken and steak were served. They complained about one of the barbers. They said she was snippy with them and gave them lousy five-minute haircuts.

Wood listened patiently, occasionally telling them that other troops had made similar points, and that changes were already in the works in some areas. He said the Academy was looking at matching each recruit with one driving instructor for the first three months, and another instructor for the second three months. He said that the Academy was thinking about closing the base barber shop and letting recruits go downtown and get their haircuts.

Most of the recruits had calendars in the trunks which they used to count the days until the end of training. Some of them kept track by how many drill classes they had left, or how many more times they had to go to the gym. Others just marked an "X" through each day, and finally the end arrived. Graduation day was the first Friday in April, and the final class was held on Thursday afternoon. It was at the Academy's range.

The recruits had been going to the range each week since they started training, and they had learned how to fire revolvers, .308-calibre bolt-action rifles and 12-gauge pump-action shotguns. They spent half of their final class learning how to secure their guns at home and how to "neutralize" firearms, which meant taking the bullets out and making sure the weapons could not be fired. They got to examine about twenty-five different guns, everything from an Uzi submachine gun, a favorite weapon of terrorists, to a zip gun which a criminal might make in a prison workshop.

The second half of the class was held in the 25-metre pistol range. The subject of the class was "shooting decisions," and it was no accident that it was the last thing they were taught. This was where they received what was arguably the most important training at the

Firearms instructor Mike Lynn watches the recruits shoot at the range.

Academy. It was where they had to make split-second decisions about whether they should pull out their guns and kill people. Statistically, they had been told, there was little chance that they would have to do it during their careers, but there was always a possibility. The subject had already been covered quite thoroughly in various ways in several other classes, but this time the lesson had a stark sense of reality.

"This is where you put it all together," Corporal Mike Lynn explained. "You have to apply all the skills you've acquired in revolver training, along with everything else you've learned in law and self-defence and operational training classes about when it's appropriate to use deadly force." Lynn had a film projector set up. He used a movie which contained various scenarios, and he projected the images onto a screen which was down in the range. The recruits used live ammunition and had to decide whether or not to shoot, depending on what they saw on the screen.

Lynn gave them a demonstration. In the filmed scenario, a call came in that shots had been fired at a gas station. The recruit was standing on the firing line, and saw the scene from the point of view of a police officer who was entering the gas station's office. Inside, a man made a quick movement, as if he were raising a gun. If the recruit decided to shoot, he would

Recruits practising firing shotguns. Statistically, there is little chance an RCMP officer will have to make a life or death decision involving firearms.

fire right through the screen. But beside the man was a second person, apparently the gas station attendant. Should the recruit shoot under those circumstances?

Lynn froze the action and said that in a split-second, the police officer would have to decided whether to fire or not. It was a tough call, and there were several factors to be considered. Could the recruit shoot straight enough the hit the robber and not hit the attendant? If he didn't shoot, would the robber shoot him? Would he have enough time to get out of the line of fire? The situation was full of "what ifs," but Lynn pointed out that the officer would have to make a quick decision. "I hope you never have to do it," he said, "but if you do, remember your skills." Then Lynn gave each of the recruits a couple of chances to make shooting decisions. After the scenario was finished, he went over what they had done, critiquing their performance and giving them tips and advice.

In one scene, the recruit's partner was stabbed by a man, who then turned and started coming toward the recruit. The trainee drew his gun, pointed it at the man and yelled at him to stop, but he didn't fire. The man kept coming and the scenario ended. Lynn told him he

Don Davidson and Kathy Furgason practise shooting stances during revolver training.

should have fired. "You had a clear field and you could have gotten off a good shot. Your partner had been stabbed and your life was in immediate danger. Lethal force was clearly justified in this case."

Another recruit was fired upon by a man driving by in a car. The recruit was slow to respond but eventually he fired at the car. He kept firing as the car sped off into the distance. "You should have fired sooner," Lynn told him, "and you shouldn't shoot at a vehicle which has moved well away from you."

In another scene, the recruit pulled over a car for speeding. The driver was belligerent and made threats as he opened the car's glove compartment, ostensibly to get his driver's licence. He pulled out a gun. The recruit pulled out his own weapon and fired just as the man was bringing the gun around towards him. Lynn said that with the benefit of hindsight, the recruit should have pulled his gun out sooner, but he noted that Mounties are less inclined to draw their weapons than American cops under such circumstances. "They get their guns out when they go to the washroom," Lynn joked. "We don't want to see police officers get like that here." This was one of those situations where Lynn said the recruit was "caught between a rock and a hard place." He couldn't overreact when the man went toward the glove compartment, but he couldn't ignore the potential threat to his safety.

Some of the scenarios put the recruits in impossible situations. One showed a boy of about eight who seemed to be innocently riding by on his bicycle. The recruit had no reason to believe he was in danger until the boy suddenly pulled a gun from under his jacket and shot at him point blank. With hindsight, Lynn said, the police officer should have drawn his gun and run for cover, but there was no way the officer could have foreseen what was coming, and cops couldn't start pointing their guns at every kid who passed by on a bike.

In one of the most interesting scenes, the recruit was responding to a call that a sniper was shooting near a railway track. He arrived and saw a man with a strange smile on his face. The man started walking toward the recruit, apparently holding something behind his back. The recruit ordered him to stop, but the man kept coming. The recruit drew his gun and ordered the man to stop, but he kept coming. The recruit aimed at the man but held his fire. The man pulled a card from behind his back. It said, "I am deaf and dumb." Lynn asked the recruit why he didn't shoot, when there was plenty of reason in this case to do so. The recruit said he didn't know why he held back. "Something just told me not to shoot." Lynn said that sometimes that's what it came down to. "You go with your instincts, and hope that they're right."

The next day was Friday, their last day at the Academy, and the recruits had a busy schedule. They had to pick up their cheques to cover their expenses for travelling to their detachments. They had to put on displays of their skills in gymnastics and self-defence, and then get dressed in their red serge uniforms and lead the noon parade. After that, they had to give a drill demonstration, take part in the graduation ceremony, and give tours of the base to their families and friends, who had come to Regina from across the country to be with them on the big day.

At night, they would celebrate at a banquet and dance. Each of the recruits had put $35 from every pay cheque while they were at the Academy into a savings account. They had accumulated about $13,000 to pay for the party, which would be attended by about 400 guests. It was like a big wedding, with twenty-seven grooms and three brides, all newly married to the RCMP. The celebration was going to be held in the drill hall, which was decorated and darkened to provide a relaxed, festive atmosphere. But before all that, they had to practise their drill routine, and that was what brought them to the drill hall at 7:30 a.m. on their final day.

Corporal Ferguson wasn't there. He had taken a couple of weeks off to go fishing with his son, and Corporal Stewart had taken over the troop. As they trickled into the drill hall, he joked with them, knowing that they were tense and that they would be under a lot of pressure on their final day. He kidded Colette Perrier about wearing too much eye makeup. "Did you put it on with an air gun?" He told Trevor MacKay that he was looking sharp, but not to let it go to his head "because there's not enough room in there."

Then he called them to attention and got down to business. Stewart wanted them to be relaxed, but not too relaxed. He knew that a troop performed best when it had just the right level of tension. If the recruits were too tight, they would fall all over themselves when they went through their complex fifteen-minute drill routine. If they were too loose, they would be sloppy and they would miss the split-second timing that was crucial to a good performance.

Stewart told them he wanted them to march with style. "It's one thing to do it mechanically like a robot," he said, "and another thing to do it with style. You want to do it smoothly, like a well-oiled machine. A lack of style shows up as nervousness on the face, jerkiness in the movements, and generally letting the jitters take over. You show that you've got style when you look calm, like you know what you're doing. You're under pressure, but you're handling the pressure."

He took the recruits through the routine which they had been working on for the past several weeks. It was a unique display. Stewart devised individual routines for each of his troops. He found that Troop 17 was an average group, so he put together a program which blended easy and difficult moves. It would challenge them, but it would not be so difficult that it would be impossible for them to do perfectly. The toughest part of the routine was a four-way cross-over called the Cross of St. Andrew.

"It's the only place where they have to act as individuals," Stewart explained. "Everywhere else, they're working as a team and doing everything in concert, but when they're doing the Cross of St. Andrew, they're in single file and they're coming from opposite directions, cutting through each other as they make the cross. Each one has to hit a certain point at a certain time. You let someone pass through the line, and then you cross, making sure you don't hit anybody. If you're half a pace off you'll run into somebody or you'll get clipped with a fist, because the arms are up swinging shoulder high. If you really blow it, you get your hat knocked off, and that looks pretty awful."

Graduation day went off without a hitch. The recruits did everything they had to, and when it came time for the drill demonstration, it was practically flawless. Nobody even came close to having his hat knocked off. After it was over, the recruits lined up in two ranks. The half-hour graduation ceremony was full of pomp and circumstance, with the officers wearing their swords and the recruits' spouses, kids, parents and friends watching proudly from the bleachers. There were so many onlookers, they spilled out onto the drill hall floor. One by one their names were called out and the graduates came up to the front and got their badges.

After the badge presentations, Dave Dubnyk went to the microphone. He was the troop's valedictorian, and he summed things up well. "As we look at today's graduating troop," he said, "it is difficult to imagine that this troop which stands so proudly before you today is the same group of young men and women who came to the Training Academy just six months ago. As grad is finally upon us, we look to the future and anxiously await what the RCMP has to offer us. To get to this point wasn't easy. Together as a troop we accomplished what we thought to be the impossible. Today, Troop 17 stands before you, shoulder to shoulder for the last time. It was not so long ago, that fateful day when Troop 17 had their first drill class right here in the hall where we stand today. We still remember that day, as we stood with fearful hearts and weak legs."

He thanked everyone who helped them become Mounties, and then Dubnyk returned to his place in the ranks. Chief Superintendent Spring formally dismissed the troop. They turned right, marched a couple of paces, and broke ranks. At that moment, Troop 17 technically ceased to exist. Officially, and finally, it was over. The recruits stood looking at one another for a moment, unsure of what they should do next. Then they drew together, shook hands and put their arms around each other. Somebody called out, "Who's the best troop?" and for one last time they replied, in a loud, strong voice, "17!" Then they broke apart and went their separate ways. Troop 17 was history.

Paul Gilligan and his son Justin at the family orientation.

For the family orientation lecture recruits attend class in full red serge for the first and only time. After this class, the Troop and their families attend a church service at the RCMP chapel.

Suzanne Lund lines up Troop 17 to take part in the Sergeant Major's Parade during graduation.

Superintendent Tony Antoniuk watches as Troop 17 goes through drill maneouvres on graduation day.

Training Academy OIC Bill Spring inspects Suzanne Lund.

Baltej Dhillon, band member and first Sikh recruit to wear a turban, appears to lead Troop 17 around the parade square. Dhillon was a member of Troop 20, a few weeks behind Troop 17 in training.

After the Sergeant Major's parade, Troop 17 marches into the drill hall for the official graduation ceremony.

After weeks of practice, Troop 17 performs Graduation Day drill routine.

OIC Bill Spring presents Suzanne Lund with her badge. As the right marker, she is the first member of Troop 17 to graduate.

Lorin Lopetinsky and Dave Rampersad congratulate each other.

Garret Hoogestraat, his son Christopher and John Babbitt celebrate a successful graduation ceremony

Graduation Master of Ceremonies John Christensen and OIC Bill Spring join in a toast.

Suzanne Lund removes Troop 17's number from the drill hall. Troop 17 no longer exists.

Troop 17's group portrait. The strings and the map indicate where each troop member has been posted.

Pat Zunti and the rest of the men's dorm pack up to leave.

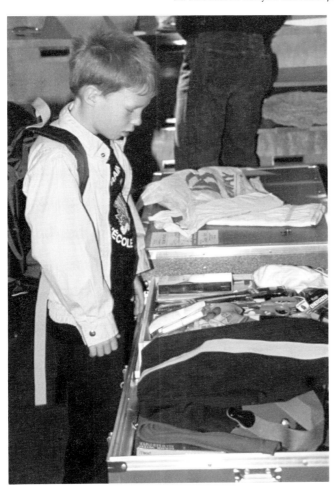

Christopher Hoogestraat contemplates his father's uniform and his new career in the RCMP.

TROOP 17